FAITH *and* SEED

Erin Daniel Bryant

ISBN 979-8-89043-399-2 (paperback)
ISBN 979-8-89043-400-5 (digital)

Christian Faith Publishing
832 Park Avenue
Meadville, PA 16335
www.christianfaithpublishing.com

All biblical citations were taken from the New International Version of the Holy Bible unless otherwise indicated.

Printed in the United States of America

MY BAPTISM

On December 3, 2019, at about 9:30 a.m., I was baptized into Christ. It was a ceremony with six of my prisoner brothers included. We were baptized by two volunteers from Calvary Chapel, Phoenix, Arizona. John Johnson was our personal friend who came every week from Calvary Chapel on Tuesdays for a Bible study class. He presided over our baptisms after a prayer and a brief testimonial from each person being baptized.

On Easter Sunday of 2019, I was watching a Christian broadcast on TV. I was overcome by the Holy Spirit and had a brief experience like a vision. I had bowed my head in tears and was contemplating my sinful past. During this contemplation, I had a profound feeling I was standing before the Lord. In this waking vision, I could see the Savior on the cross before me with his hands and feet pierced. I was crushed. I spent the evening in prayer and studying Scripture. That day, I decided I would ask to be baptized. I mentioned my desire to John sometime in the following months. Eventually, baptisms were scheduled, and the other men from Bible studies were baptized as well.

We were joyful to declare Jesus Christ our Lord and Savior. The baptisms were done in a one-man tub fashioned of a canvas overlay fold-out tub provided to the prison by an organization called ARM Prison Outreach. Leading up to our baptisms, we had all shared Bible studies with John. Many prisoners here have been greatly blessed by the fellowship and prayers along with studies.

Before my calling and new life in Christ, I have been incarcerated many times. I will be released after serving eight years in prison for a current charge. I have been incarcerated for a total of seventeen years. I was first incarcerated for auto theft at nineteen years old and served three years. I have been in Douglas Complex, Gila Unit. I have been in SMU 2 in the Central Unit, known as the Walls. I have been in Kingman, Cerbat Unit, and presently in Cibola Unit, Yuma, Arizona. It has been such a hard road, and I am really blessed to have God's mercies! I can know without a doubt it is his miracles that have brought me to repentance. Every day is a new blessing for me to share a testimony with any who will hear of our Savior.

On Easter Sunday of 2021, about fifteen of my prisoner brothers in the pod shared the body and blood of our Lord. We came together in the center of the pod, building 6, A and B pod. In reverence and praise, we prayed, broke bread, and made small cups of grape Kool-Aid. We began with an opening reading of Isaiah 51. It was deeply humbling to share and to see these men, even in this place, as hardened criminals, graciously remembering the Savior together on Easter with the sacrament. I know miracles happen through the Holy Spirit and Jesus every day! I am a living testimony of his grace!

CHAPTER 1

Faith and the Seed

As a man who has been lost and to whom the gospel of faith in Christ is the greatest treasure I have ever discovered, I would like to share the story of my own redemption from the hand of the enemy.

"Let the redeemed of the Lord tell their story, those He redeemed from the hand of the foe" (Psalm 107:2 NIV).

This is a time of true hardship in my life. My current situation is a trial and a tribulation of seemingly insurmountable size. In the middle of this travail—in prison, with relief escaping me—a tiny seed of faith began to grow in my heart. With just one spark of God's light, a bright and vibrant glow started inside my heart. A prayer, a Bible, and a year later, a brand-new man has been born. I came to realize that through this experience, God was building my heart upon his Word. The Lord God of the world is powerful to save and restore a person in every way. His Word can straighten a man and plant his feet on the solid rock of Christ's salvation.

My purpose in writing this book is to display the light of the gospel of Jesus Christ. His life and sacrifice bring hope to the lost, faith to the faithless, life to the spiritually dead, and truth to those who have been deceived. My prayer is for salvation from our Lord for those who have not yet received his Son, Jesus Christ. My prayer is for the washing and regeneration of their soul, through the Holy Spirit, for all who receive Christ in their hearts.

Through this experience, I've come to know the basic principles of the gospel as invaluable tools. Tools of profound importance are essential to a life of freedom in this very troublesome world. My story is one of hope, victory, and spiritual freedom while in the middle of this storm. It is born in the middle of extreme circumstances. In prison, because of a sinful life, the light of our Savior reaches into the darkness. His light reached into my heart and mind—a violent criminal and even into this damaged soul of a scoundrel. There I was looking into the mirror as a five-time convicted felon, hopeless!

The ambition of this effort is not to sensationalize or glorify my past life. The details of my actions and my current prison situation will be concise; they are very real results of my sinful nature. While here in the Arizona Department of Corrections, I have learned about immeasurable peace in the rest of our Lord and Savior, Jesus Christ. I am currently serving an eight-and-a-half-year sentence for a violent crime. In one fearful moment, I attacked and caused severe injury to a man who had pulled a knife on me. His forehead and face were cut, and his left ear was nearly severed completely from his head. I am guilty of so many awful things. So many people have been harmed because of me, and I had no hope of wiping the stain of shame and disgrace from my heart and soul without the words of Jesus Christ.

> Jesus answered, "Everyone who drinks
> this water will be thirsty again, but whoever
> drinks the water I give them will never thirst.
> Indeed, the water I give them will become in

them a spring of water welling up to eternal
life." (John 4:13–14 NIV)

As I read these words of our Savior, the Holy Spirit of God began to pour this life-giving water upon the seed of faith that has been in my heart. The seed is now firmly planted by all of the words I have heard and read about Jesus Christ.

"For God so loved the world that He gave His one and only Son, that whoever believes in Him shall not perish but have eternal life" (John 3:16 NIV).

These verses are absolutely critical in the pivotal change in my life that has become new life after repentance. In the days of my life, I have known what it means to be *thirsty*. Jesus was telling the Samaritan woman at the well about her condition. She was spiritually as thirsty as a person would be after a week with no water, like a desert without a single thing that can grow.

I know what it is to thirst. My boyhood and teenage years were never lacking in desperation and the constant pursuit of something to fill that empty place inside. Those years were full of tangled webwork of lies, deceit, violence, and theft. At the age of fourteen, I was first arrested and later convicted for my first felony burglary. This was the inevitable transitional event that catapulted me into further evil. It was also the event that marked me on the inside, warping any sense of esteem I had before that point.

My life took a much darker course from that point on. In my fifteenth year of life, a few months before my sixteenth birthday, I packed a backpack and left my family and home behind. Thirsty is a good description of my life. From my heart and soul to the bottoms of my feet, I knew the anxious trepidation of being in a frenzy of physical and emotional *thirst*. Now with the life of Christ born inside me, I know it all stemmed from being dead spiritually.

In those years of my life, I was thirsty for any relief. No food, relationship, community, event, or anything at all could have ever had the power to fill that void. My continued search was more of the same anxious thirsty feeling. It is a feeling only the Lord can cure. The hopeless, vain, and empty life is the whole nature of a person without the watered seed of Jesus Christ's words, waiting to be planted and grow into an amazing tree within our hearts. He is the tree of life that grows in our lives and causes us to flourish in peace, love, patience, kindness, and truth. Those years of waste and desolation were the result of a heart that needed Christ to be renewed.

Some people may not experience the same extreme physical circumstances that I have, but I assure you the very same thirst for the inner sustenance our souls desire is still there. Here I am, forty-one years old in prison for eight and a half years, and *I* am a person Christ has given the living water to. Why in the world would God want to give me anything good at all? Why? Now you must take into consideration that the question *why* is preceded by my guilt. I am a deadbeat dad with two sons who have really never had a real father. I am a man whose ex-wife is broken by our awful divorce.

Take into account that I am a divorced deadbeat dad, a lifelong criminal, and a prisoner; and ask yourself why I would want to accept that neither God nor a man would want to give me anything good at all. Why would God want to give a criminal who has been in both the newspaper and TV news for numerous crimes anything good?

There is one very simple and amazingly profound reason. In this world of pain and wickedness, suffering, grief, and confusion—*thirst*, affliction upon affliction—the God of Heaven is good. He is so good and simply wants to give us all good things. You may think what I once thought, *Unless I can figure out how to do better first, none of that goodness is really for me. If I use com-*

mon sense, for instance, I know good from bad. Try as I may, I can never really achieve the devotion and character necessary to do all that I know is right, let alone be able to do all that Jesus Christ and God the Father have told me is right.

I now know it has been given to me by God. This new birth of the Holy Spirit gives light to guide me out of spiritual darkness. How do I find the faith to believe in any of God's goodness, especially to believe it is for me? It all begins with the seed and how it is planted in all of our hearts. The seed is the word of God that comes to us through Christ.

"Faith comes by hearing the message, and the message is heard by the word of God" (Romans 10:17 NIV).

In the very dawn of this new life as a born-again Christian, while here in prison, God began to transform me. His Holy Spirit, alive within my soul, gave life to what was once dead. This is the essence of what our God is; He is the life that is eternal. When we stumble and fall into the devastation of sinfulness, we know terrible pain. When we know we are not following all of God's commands in our lives, do we then die again to God? Are we those who, because of our sin, are brought under condemnation?

In my own life, while living in my own strength and as a man guilty of so much sin, my answer to those questions would have been only the answers of my own evil heart. My answer would probably have been something like this: "I'm not keeping the words of the Lord right now, I'm going to end up in hell." And I would have been right, not because of any sinful thing that prohibits me from being saved from hell; the problem was the sin of unbelief. My beliefs were all wrong! I have come to know through the word of God contained in the Holy Bible that hell and condemnation are only for those who do not believe in Jesus Christ and the promises God made to mankind through him.

Why was I unable to know that my salvation was already secure if I wanted it? Was it my sin that blocked the seed of God's word from growing within me? Was it because I'm just a man with a mind incapable of enough faith? Was it because my heart is too evil? Was it because I simply failed to change enough bad behaviors into good behaviors? In all of these simple questions, there is one resounding similarity. They are all questions that point to the same thing. They all center around me.

All of the hindrances inside of the hungry heart and soul of a man come from inside of us—all of our own wisdom, ideas, and life experiences, which include all of our efforts to do good things. These things are ineffective to gratify our yearning soul; instead, they are all ingredients that amplify the astounding desire we have for God's love within us. We are still thirsty.

When a man or a woman is unaware of the word of God, there is an unquenchable thirst. It's an empty life even if it's full of the successes of our efforts. That is the existence of a man or a woman who has not received the Savior into their hearts. The most profound lesson of all is it never started with me doing enough anyway. It all started with *him*—the Lord and Savior of all who come to God through him and accept his free gift of salvation.

There I was in surrender to every evil force, including all of my own efforts to do good. I know I was completely clueless. Then sitting in my anguish, fear, depression, and grief, the God of all creation began a new work in me simply by speaking to me through the word of his mouth—every word of the Holy Bible.

I had been a believer before for a time, or so I thought. I spent about four years as a member of the Church of Jesus Christ of Latter-day Saints. In this religion, I had been very dedicated to striving to do all the things they taught me. At one point in my service as an elder, I was a teacher at a Sunday service and also was called a missionary. I had strong beliefs and lots of duties and even baptized two people.

The four years of participation in the Mormon church were a decent lifestyle. I must say it was a blessed time of my life. It was much better than the times I had been in prison, better than life without community, devotion, and duty. I was blessed with an intelligent woman for a wife—a very beautiful brunette who had a career as a teacher. She was a graduate with degrees in physics and chemistry. We were blessed with a new baby boy together. Then divorce and devastation tore the rug of illusion out from underneath me.

What in all the world could have gone wrong? I found myself in a desert with that desperate parched feeling in my soul, asking all of the same ageless timeless questions: Was it because I had sinned too much, because the faith I had nourished for four years was simply too weak, or because I had failed to change enough negative behaviors to better behaviors?

Once again, the exact same problem is evident. All of the questions have *me* in the center. Now with the Lord and Savior Jesus Christ in the center, I understand what the sure foundation is. He is the foundation for salvation. The problem of the human heart and soul in its *thirst* is impossible to solve from the *me* foundation. And no, the *me* foundation is not a nonprofit organization.

Why? After all, the four years of devotion to my church brothers and sisters were good. I thought that I knew the gospel in a very deep and sincere way. For a time, I had practiced complete abstinence from alcohol and even caffeine. All the systems and even random solutions that seem to fit are wrong. All of the yearnings and dreams that are fruitless enter into the mind and heart because it is not being filled with the *living water* of God's Holy Spirit. We must be fed by the bread of our Savior's Word.

Simply enough, the Lord invested himself into me with the word of his mouth. The scriptures contained in the Holy Bible have prospered in my heart, mind, body, and soul. He has taken from me all the beliefs and ideas I was overwhelmed by. His Word has taken the experiences I once thought defined the end result, causing me to realize all my personal efforts to change bad behavior needed him. It all started with him, his faith.

All I did was pray for God's help, ask for forgiveness, and begin to read and study the Bible. A miracle occurred right here in prison. All the garbage in my heart, mind, and actions started to be cleaned.

"You are already clean because of the word I have spoken to you" (John 15:3 NIV).

"Wait just one moment there, buddy, you haven't even changed one single thing"—that is exactly what the first attacks of the enemy were like. My own fool's thoughts tried to steal the seeds of faith Christ had sown into my heart. All my past ideas were built upon the supposed fact that my own actions were the big game changer. The notion that I had to force myself to have better actions in life or to behave up to some standard of conduct was a constant snare to me in my new life in Christ.

You are probably thinking, *Doesn't God want a person to have good actions or to work on changing his or her behaviors?* In the beginning of this born-again Christian transformation, I thought my cigarette habit had to stop or I would be someone who doesn't really have salvation. I had no idea in what way or when or how God was working.

"As the heavens are higher than the earth, so are my ways higher than your ways and my thoughts than your thoughts" (Isaiah 55:9 NIV).

Was it at all possible that my sinful actions are not an island I am stuck on or a dam, something that would stop him from knowing me? How is it that all my sins don't stop me dead in my tracks? Stranded—it was a simple answer. I had the insurmountable obstacle of my own conscience simply because all of my past beliefs were ultimately wrong. As I continue to prayerfully read and study the words of our Savior, *his faith* has been planted in my heart. God's seed is strengthened, invigorated, and nourished into continual growth when it is fed by the words of Jesus Christ. This is the natural essential quality of God's work. His holiness remains perfect even when I am nowhere near perfect. The enemy of God, the deceiver, the king of lies wants to use my sins and imperfections to try to destroy God's work being done within me. He tries to instigate me into judging myself falsely to blind me, using any of my efforts to do better against me because of all errors or sins I may still have.

If Satan—in his lies and schemes—can manipulate me into believing I am not doing good enough, he gains control. If Satan can convince me into believing I have to do more than what God has already done for me through his Son, he can lead me to build upon the false foundation of my own works. Here is an example: "I fear I may not really have salvation or eternal life or even forgiveness on account of my smoking. I am afraid I will be judged even though I believe in the Son of God and the promises he made to me."

When a person has these thoughts, it feels as if smoking must stop or we will still be condemned. In the heart or mind of a person who is not being fed by the word of God, that idea is the destroyer of God's gift of grace to us.

It is always the work of the enemy to attack the seed of faith God has sown in us simply by turning our faith in Christ instead to our own good efforts or our lack of good efforts. He can trick us into building on a false foundation. Here is the question answered by Christ as to what my predicament with God is if I believe in his Words.

Then he turned toward the woman and said to Simon, "Do you see this woman? I came into your house. You did not give me any water for my feet, but she wet my feet with her tears and wiped them with her hair. You did not give me a kiss, but this woman, from the time I entered, has not stopped kissing my feet. You did not put oil on my head, but she has poured perfume on my feet. Therefore, I tell you, her many sins have been forgiven—as her great love has shown. But whoever has been forgiven little loves little." (Luke 7:44–47 NIV)

In the above verses, Christ addresses a person's works, efforts, and even sin. The woman was described in the verses before this verse as a sinful woman. She exhibited her love in both humble and simple actions. In her efforts of love, she washed his feet and wiped them with her hair. Her adoration was work enough, and our savior accepted her even in her sinful nature. There was no mention of the woman being anyone who in any way had stopped herself from sinful ways. She placed her faith and love upon the Son of God.

"Jesus said to the woman, "Your faith has saved you; go in peace" (Luke 7:50 NIV).

After the new birth of the Holy Spirit within me because of the words of Christ, the importance of my own works is washed away by the cleansing blood of my savior. His work is being done in me. The old useless dead foundation has been replaced by the sure foundation of Jesus Christ.

The purpose of Christ being sacrificed is for the hope of mankind to be saved. We can have peace, love, and truth in Christ's sacrifice, resurrection, and eternal life. The inner man is healed by him. When he is our faith, the destructive things we have experienced—whether it is sin or confusion or any of our human sinful conditions—are no longer the determiner of our lives. Instead of these human frailties, we are now the newly germinating seeds that grow into a new creation.

"For you have been born again, not of perishable seed, but of imperishable, through the living and enduring word of God" (1 Peter 1:23 NIV).

And this is the very beginning of the miracle of God within us.

CHAPTER 2

Inner Man of the Holy Spirit

In order for the grace and power of God to heal the inner man or woman, the Holy Spirit must be trusted as an extension of God the Father. All of us who are given the blessing of God's hand in our lives have been drawn by the Father to his Son, Jesus Christ. We are given many blessings from God, including eternal promises. One promise to us is also the primary purpose of our God—to fulfill his desire that we become his children. In the words of John, the disciple, this is made very clear as a pivotal part of God's plan to heal us by his Word and to be a father to us.

> Yet to all who did receive Him, to these who believed in His name, He gave the right to become children of God—children born not of natural descent, or human decision or a husband's will, but born of God. (John 1:12, 13 NIV)

As his children, born of his spirit through our faith in his Son, Jesus Christ, we have the blessing of his fatherhood. We can know we are those who can be healed completely. Every one of us has had to endure many injuries to the mind, heart, and soul. Do these injuries—whether it be injustice, betrayal, or even sickness or calamity—stand in the way of our contentment or hope? It may be the damages we've inflicted upon ourselves or others because of sinful habits or even downfalls caused by confusion or possible trauma or family issues—whatever the nature of these injuries may be. More important than the injuries themselves, the spirit of God has revealed a simple truth to me that these may be what is being held inside of the heart instead of being filled by the Holy Spirit of our Lord.

When his faith ignites upon us, our hearts are filled with his hope of healing for us. In the rebirth through the Holy Spirit, we are born of God by his imperishable seed, Jesus Christ, as God's Word is the seed. He begins to live through us, and we no longer have to remain in the guilt that has held us captive to the pain, whatever it may be that has brought us into the darkness and despair—whether it's been abuse, divorce, addiction, or multiple problems. Whatever the existing damages we have been afflicted with, all of our life experiences are an accumulation of *perishable seed*, just as the disciple Peter wrote about. We are called into the covenant of God's grace. With the gospel of Jesus Christ, God's perfect truth has won the victory over those dead perishable things.

Wherever we may be in life, even in dire straits, we are now the new creations of God. The pain and sorrow being the perishable things of our lives begin to be transformed by God's Word. As our childhood to our Heavenly Father goes forward and we are fed by his Word, we begin to grow up into our salvation. When we receive this imperishable seed from our Savior Jesus Christ, it is accompanied by the Holy Spirit of our Lord. We are in the image of God, his spirit children. As we read the Bible and the Savior's Words begin to grow within us, we are made clean.

"You are already clean, because of the word I have spoken to you" (John 15:3 NIV).

In this simple and profound statement, we find ourselves in the glory from above. In this very important principle of God's faithfulness to us, we find victory over our own weakened, impoverished human hearts and souls. We can now be nourished by God's living Word and continuously be refreshed and cleaned by his Holy Spirit. With a grain of faith the size of a mustard seed in our hearts, the dead desolation inside our mind and soul is surely replaced by our new life in God's Son, Jesus Christ.

If there is a past offense done to you, you must forgive it in order for the healing of our Savior to happen. An impoverishment of our soul is extremely painful, a dark abyss without the light of Christ. The Lord can heal our weakened human soul and light up the darkest emotional abyss with his Holy Spirit. Any kind of resentment in our hearts and minds will cause us to experience a wide range of negative attitudes and emotions. We cannot sow the perishable seeds of our human souls and hearts and expect to reap anything other than additional negativity and pain.

When we allow the new creation that has been born within us through our Lord's imperishable seed to grow, we will now be those who are sharing in the peace of our Lord and Savior, Jesus Christ.

"Peace I leave with you; my peace I give you. I do not give to you as the world gives. Do not let your hearts be troubled and do not be afraid" (John 14:27 NIV).

Peace is the outcome of the Holy Spirit's power within us. We are now the children of God, and we too begin to sow seed with him. The imperishable perfect seed of our Savior's Word bears its fruit within us. It flows over into the world that surrounds us in the form of forgiveness, mercy, hope, and love.

When these are the Holy Spirit's blessings with us and through Christ we are alive to them, there will be no place for the unforgiven offense. The spirit of light has no fellowship with darkness.

"The light shines in the darkness, and the darkness has not overcome it" (John 1:5 NIV).

When we are focused on blaming anyone for anything, we may feel that we are right to do so. For instance, if a spouse has an affair, it may feel right to blame the person for the pain and sorrow—this being our human logic. For example, it only hurts because they had an affair and were deceptive. If this is true, how do we find healing for the pain? The Lord Jesus Christ who is the living Word of God gives us his promise. His promise is to become God's children through faith in him.

If the cost of my own sins were paid for on the cross of Calvary, I am one of those he purchased with his own blood! This means my heart should be turned to him. We know our Savior prayed for the people who killed him, accused him, blamed him falsely, and hated him. We also, as people who have all sinned, are directly responsible for the Son of God being slain as a sacrifice. This is the conviction of sin in a disciple of Jesus Christ.

With this knowledge brought to my heart through the miracle of the Holy Spirit, I am now a man with a renewed heart. The Savior is alive within me, and now I can enjoy the peace of communion with our God. All of God's healing miracles now transform my old broken heart into a new heart.

The damages once done to my soul because of sin—my own sin—or that of others can be healed. The inner man born of God's spirit is made brand-new. Old things are gone, and new things come to pass. This means that the wounded heart—full of false blame, accusation, fear, and hate—is gone.

The very simple truth of our Savior that has given me faith and hope has destroyed all of the perishable things that cannot enter into his presence. We must be born again in the Holy Spirit just as our Savior Jesus Christ asked of us. He was the victory over sin who conquered death in his resurrection in order for us to be justified in him. When asked by Nicodemus how someone who is already old can be born again, this is what he was told:

> Jesus answered, "Very truly I tell you, no one can enter the kingdom of God unless they are born of water and the Spirit. Flesh gives birth to flesh, but the Spirit gives birth to spirit." (John 3:5, 6 NIV)

This is a pure and simple truth of salvation. Salvation is for us to accept right now! Before we ever experience physical death, we are reborn into the life of Jesus Christ through the spirit of God. The waters of baptism are a symbol of our old lives being buried with Christ. It is also a symbol of our new birth in the resurrection of our Lord and Savior through the spirit of God. In Christ, we are made alive to God and considered dead to the evils of the world. If we are born again by water and spirit. What is the water? The perfect Son of God, Jesus Christ, promised us in the Gospel of John, the disciple, that he could give us the living water.

"But whoever drinks the water I give them will never thirst. Indeed the water I give them will become in them a spring of water welling up to eternal life" (John 4:14 NIV).

God's spirit is the pure water of Jesus Christ's Word, which can purify our souls. Just as his Word is the power in us that can well up to eternal life, the spirit of God is also born within us. His spirit is able to lead us into paths of righteousness.

These miracles are the foundation for the new Christian and the renewed Christian to be healed of any emotional scars.

With the promises made true to me through God's perfect witness, his Holy Spirit, I am healed. I have also been promised that I am God's child and, with that, inherit eternal life. With this victory in my heart and soul, I have no more worldly sorrows about any harm in my past.

"Godly sorrow brings repentance that leads to salvation and leaves no regret, but worldly sorrow brings death" (2 Corinthians 7:10 NIV).

When once the perishable seed of the natural man would have spoken death to me by saying, "You are a five-time convicted felon, your life is ruined, and you're in prison for the next eight and a half years." Now the Holy Spirit of God speaks life to me, "You are a child of the Most High God, and the living water of my Word will be a spring inside of you, which wells up to eternal life." This is the hope of the faithful, and I simply see that eternal life cannot be ruined. I am blessed to be here in ADOC. I am very blessed to be alive in the Spirit.

The good news cannot be ruined, and a disciple of Christ cannot be ruined if he has been reborn. God has revealed his truth through the Holy Spirit; all that was ruined has been destroyed. The time Christ spoke about is here for me; even in prison, I can worship the Father in spirit and truth, just as Jesus told the Samaritan woman at the well of Jacob.

"Yet a time is coming and has now come when the true worshipers will worship the Father in the spirit and in truth, for they are the kind of worshipers the Father seeks" (John 4:23 NIV).

CHAPTER 3

Repentance through Worship

The trials of our lives are continuously upon us in this world. I may be a new Christian who was just baptized here in prison, and you may be in an entirely different circumstance. Whatever our differences, however extreme the circumstances may be, all of us are troubled in the hard parts of life. This world is so full of evil that it is impossible not to be impacted by the sting of it. In the middle of what may feel like a living hell here in prison, I have grown to be grateful for it all through my worship of God. My heart is happier, and the anxieties are forgotten when I am calling out to God and giving him the glory.

The transformation of attitudes that are negative into positive ones comes freely from God through worship. Worshiping God keeps me full of positive energy during all of the chaos that surrounds me here in prison. When the Lord hears our hearts singing out to him, he reflects back at us with awesome love. With all of the violence and negative attitudes and constant noise here in prison, it is not an easy task to have any peace or hope. With a heart of worship, it is possible to have both peace and hope in abundance. In this situation, praise and worship is the most effective way to bring life into a very bleak and hopeless place.

Obedience to our God is ignited when we honor him with our worship. It is impossible to be in service to our sins while worshiping God. It is very simply an instantaneous shift in our heart's desire. The action of honoring God with songs, prayers, and preaching removes us from being in service to ourselves or any sin. Worshiping God is a sure way to feel God perfecting our hearts.

The gospel of Jesus Christ is the only sure place for the *old life* to die and the new life to begin. It is beyond anything we could ever do without Jesus. I have been blessed so greatly to know him and to leave myself behind and lie in him. When I praise him and receive his guiding light, my heart is a repentant heart. His own amazing works resound inside of my soul because he is the great *I Am.* The depth of darkness and pain is wiped clean. The hopeful mind is renewed, and the faithfulness he has for me is here within me.

The miracles of Jesus Christ are here inside of me to know and hold dear. Through him, all who are weary can be given inner strength to press forward. The obstacles of this life can be happily endured and overcome with courage and honor. With our faith and worship in him, all things become possible. He is the *victory*, and we—in turn—are his victory. When the darkness of grief and tragedy occurs even when our own sins seem to be impossible to change, God's gifts to us set our souls *free.* We struggle, we confess through worship, and we proclaim our *need* for God's wealth of mercy and hope to reflect back from within us. In his Son, Jesus Christ, our God has prepared for us perfect promises that can never be destroyed.

The enemy of God and his people would have you believe that you are lost because of all of your sins, failures, or problems. Our Savior gave us his promise. Our own humanity, weakness, and sins do not have the power to destroy his promise. No matter how much we get wrong, if we have faith to believe in his

Word to us, we will not be lost. When we worship God through his Son, Jesus Christ, he has already done what we people could never do. He *conquered* every sin even unto his death *to save us*.

> For I have come down from Heaven not to do my will but to do the will of Him who sent me. And this is the will of Him who sent me, that I shall lose none at all those that He has given me, but raise them up at the last day. For my Father's will is that everyone who looks to the Son and believes in Him shall have eternal life, and I will raise them up at the last day. (John 6:38–40 NIV)

By the very words of our Savior, just to look to him and believe in him is to be one of his sheep. His sheep will not be lost but will be saved. To be saved is also to be given eternal life. This fact is a platform from which our faith can be developed by God. In Christ, our labor and travails are no longer merely human efforts. The spirit of our God ignites the aspirations that once lay dormant. We can know his infinite potential because our human souls are now made alive with the perfect Son of God within us.

In his spirit, the divisions of strife and confusion are no longer the destroyers they once were to us. With the promises of God's faithful Son to us, faith is now a tool to be used and sharpened by the Holy Spirit. What once defeated us in our thoughts and attitudes is now the storm that is in the world around us. God gives us the wings of an eagle—faith in his Son—to fly through any storm. We are no longer grounded by fear or hopelessness, merely waiting our turn to prevail. We are able through our worship of Christ to be the prevailing force against the storm itself. The ambition to be free is not lost in obscurity, it is manifested in the life of our Savior.

"I am the way and the truth and the life. No one comes to the Father except through me" (John 14:6 NIV).

When this is the knowledge we have in our hearts, with our bodies and our souls, we are worshiping and adoring our Savior. We can know we have full and perfect access to the Father. This is the method by which I have come to know repentance through worship.

I have had so many issues, problems, and unresolved sins in my life. If the concept of salvation was to overcome my sinful condition first, and then know the Lord, I would remain lost. That is the false foundation of my old belief.

The sure foundation is the works of our God and his only perfect Son. In the gospel of Jesus Christ are contained all of the treasures of heaven. The Word of God is alive, and the miracles become vibrant lights to guide us through all things.

Here I am incarcerated for the next eight and half years without normal freedoms and liberties. I have lost my freedom, my wife, and my son. I have lost everything to gain eternal life. Believe me, when I testify in God's own spirit, I am celebrating the victory Jesus Christ won for me at Calvary. I am a "new creation" because of what he did for me. The Alpha and the Omega—the great *I Am* is my own personal friend! When the tears come flowing down my face, they are no longer tears of regret or frustration. They are now the tears of godly sorrow that are liberating to free the soul and leave me with peace, love, and unbelievable happiness.

This is all because of the work of God through faith in his Word. The constant study of Scripture is the paramount objective in the heart of worship. Scripture is the conversation of God to us, which inspires conversion. Conversion is a journey of the heart and soul into the living Word of God.

As I continue to write and describe the conversion that I have experienced through the study of the living Word, I will explain the principles I learned of the truth contained in the Bible. These truths are the most valuable treasures, pure gold, sacred diadems, refined in God's holy fire—the most valuable possession, more worthy than anything a man can buy. The gifts from God are eternal.

Once again, my life is one of pain, suffering, and experiences of tragedy and grief. During this time of discovery, there is a profound change within me. Unlike any other force that has ever been active in my life. The Holy Spirit makes me aware. First of all, my mind is already full of all the things I have known—harmful, damaging, and sinful ideas and experiences. This was all so normal to me that it didn't even seem to be the root cause of all my problems.

This brings me to what our Savior did for us. In his work for God and us, Christ reconciled our old evil nature to God so we could be made into new creations. His works begin within us to draw us closer to him. This is a miracle—changing all my evil ways, struggling not to use drugs, and struggling not to be violent. Whatever my efforts were to do good in life had absolutely no value to bring about repentance. Without the gospel of truth and the new birth in the spirit of God, the efforts were my own. True discipleship to Christ is the miracle, and it is the way to repentance.

When the God of truth is within us and his spirit pierces us to the heart, his light shines into our darkened sinful souls, and the foundation becomes his sure foundation. And from this place, the miracle of having a new mind, body, and soul begins.

> Therefore if anyone is in Christ, the new
> creation has come. The old is gone, the new
> is here! All this is from God, who reconciled

us to himself through Christ and gave us the ministry of reconciliation. (2 Corinthians 5:17–18 NIV)

Notice how God reconciled me or you to himself through Christ. God did not reconcile himself to me through my own efforts. This is a very profound truth, which means I can start this new journey in life just the way I am! I no longer feel anxious over what sins I am guilty of or a fearful dread over how or what I need to do. I am still obviously a sinner; my need for the Savior is greater than ever! Knowing Jesus Christ is the dawn of a brand-new horizon full of light. Like a brokenhearted child unable to feed himself, I am without any power at all of my own. God feeds me with the pure milk of his Word. My soul hungers for his spirit, and his Word begins to fill me with hope. What I once was is what he removed from me with his supernatural force of love.

This kind of love, so powerful it brings me to tears, is the voice of God. What I have done no longer really matters, it is what he has done for me that matters! His love is for me; it no longer has any hindrance whatsoever. He has no accusation against me. My weaknesses and failings are not held against me. This turns my heart and mind in awe toward God with a new trust in him. I am simply not in any trouble with him.

"That God was reconciling the world to himself in Christ, not counting people's sins against them. And He has committed to us the message of reconciliation" (2 Corinthians 5:19 NIV).

What an amazingly absurd idea, it has no place in my old logical thinking! I don't have to focus and dread things that God may be angry at me about. It is truly a message, unlike anything that comes from this world. Now I know what it means to be in the world but not of the world. A born-again Christian is reborn in our Savior Jesus Christ. So now, I am of the Savior Jesus Christ, and in him, the Father sees no sin!

"God made Him who had no sin to be sin for us, that in Him we might become the righteousness of God" (2 Corinthian 5:21 NIV).

What can a man like me who is a forty-one-year-old convicted felon do to claim righteousness? How could anything I am able to do or to be while here in prison be counted as good? How in any logical way do I claim I am righteous in God's eyes? Well, the answer isn't very logical at all, the truth of the gospel is understood through his spirit; it cannot be understood by a natural man. I am a convicted felon in prison, and simultaneously, I am also the righteousness of God in Christ. At this point, I cannot possibly claim I have righteous efforts outside of Christ at all! Nothing at all can be done in my own strength that is good whatsoever. The knowledge of salvation is secured by his grace. Along with it comes an increase in his intrinsic qualities—peace, hope, and love!

"But grow in the knowledge of our Lord and Savior Jesus Christ. To Him be glory both now and forever, Amen" (2 Peter 3:18 NIV).

The point is, my faith isn't *mine* at all, it is the faith of our Lord within me. Worship in the form of prayer, singing, and reading his Word is the epitome of turning to God. Repentance starts here. God's glory is being praised. His works are glorified, and the faith in my heart is for him.

In worship, the confession of Christ as our Savior is demonstrated. His majesty is proclaimed, and the resurrection is celebrated. These actions keep our eyes pointed toward the Lord.

This is how worship brought me to my feet in Christ's victory. Repentance through worship brought me up off my prayerful knees of confusion, fear, hate, regret, resentment, anger, and hopelessness. My worship is an action the Lord accepted and reflected back at me with love. In his love for me, the scriptures opened up in a brand-new way. They became *alive*!

CHAPTER 4

Faith before Works

The new life in Christ is spirit-filled and enables me to walk in his power. This power is cutting like a sword of truth through confusion. There is always so much that we need to be able to adapt to in this life; awareness of God's spirit sharpens our minds. The word of the Holy Bible is clear: we are being tempered by him. With the darkness of Satan's efforts to destroy us with sin, unbelief, lies, and false doctrines, we need gratitude for the words of our Savior Jesus Christ. His teachings are a power within us to cut through all lies and deception. The enemy's efforts to deceive and destroy, seeking to diminish us as we fill up on God's Word, are defeated.

When we are made aware in the spirit of Christ by his words, we are saved, not by any other means except by him. When trepidation or a shadow of doubt enters our hearts for any reason, we can know it is not of Christ. So here I am guilty of so much sin, still even struggling and being conscious of sins that remain as yet unchanged. This is the trial of my belief—to keep his faith with strength and hold fast to his truth. Satan is always in an effort to deceive us into judgment because we are in a struggle with our own sin.

During all of this, the spirit of God is with us from within to disarm the power of evil around us. The Spirit is with us to bear witness to the Son of God and what he has done for us. False teachings, evil people, and evil spirits are all very real. So much of our pain results directly from the devil's efforts to destroy us. It is of the utmost importance to be filled with Christ's Word to be able to see the enemy's lies. We can be cleansed from the pain and despair that are caused by the devil's schemes and the attacks against our minds.

I have yet many weaknesses and unresolved problems, as well as sins; this is common. It is not the difference between good and bad works. True gospel teachings dispel the doubt that would otherwise destroy true faith in him. Very simply, these are the human things that come from the flesh. We have a promise from him, which is to be in him through faith. This allows us to do good works through him and to bear good fruits, not because of what we do but because of what he does through us! The stumbling block and the pitfall of doubt are gone.

Despite our own pitiful human downfalls, we can still do his will and bear good fruits because our works are alive in him. In other words, I am a sinner in prison for committing a violent crime, so how can I possibly do any good work for our Lord while still in this condition? That was an old belief that has since been buried with Christ, and a new life has been born in his infinite spirit. Without any idea of my own efforts or works in the way, I could not be *born again* in him to do righteousness at all. I can only bear fruit with faith *in him*.

> I am the vine; you are the branches. If you remain in me and I in you, you will bear much fruit; apart from me you can do noth-ing. If you do not remain in me, you are like a branch that is thrown away and withers; such

branches are picked up, thrown into the fire
and burned. (John 15:5, 6 NIV)

So I now have an answer from our Savior Jesus Christ to dispel any doubts about whether or not I can do good works. By faith in him, this is possible. All of the words of the Holy Bible are critically important to the rebirth we have as Christians. The study of the Bible is fundamental for the restorative power of God to work in our lives. Empowerment through the holy scriptures is the force within us to bring regeneration to our bodies, minds, hearts, and souls. The living water Jesus spoke of is a representation of the Holy Spirit. The Holy Spirit through God's Word is what a born-again Christian's soul yearns for.

"Like newborn babies, crave pure spiritual milk, so that by it you may grow up in your salvation" (1 Peter 2:2 NIV).

When the Holy Spirit of God is within us as we read and learn, we begin to literally grow up into our salvation. From the Holy Bible, true gospel principles are being sown directly from the Lord into our lives. Miracles begin to occur inside of us and in the world around us. My personal testimony is a witness to God's regenerative power that restored my mind to sanity. My darkened negative attitudes once laden with jaded criticism, scorn, and evil judgments have been transformed. God's Word and his Holy Spirit have changed those ideas from my old evil nature into faith-filled hopes and wholesome ambitions.

In my life as a prisoner, this pivotal change in my attitude is most definitely a miracle. This new mind is provided to any of us with faith in our Savior Jesus Christ. Here in prison—surrounded by pessimism, hopelessness, hate, grief, fear, and all sorts of miseries—God fills my mind with his goodness. In the Holy Bible, principles such as repentance have been made crystal clear. Any and all doubts we may have in regard to our own inability to do what God has asked of us are removed by the holy scriptures.

We can simply come to God through his Son, Jesus Christ, in the confession of our sins and ask for his mercy! Humility is a principle sown into our hearts through God's Word, and confession along with repentance to God is best done in humility.

> To some who were confident of their own righteousness and looked down on everyone else, Jesus told this parable, "The Pharisee and the other a tax collector. The Pharisee stood by himself and prayed, 'God I thank you that I am not like other people—robbers, evildoers, adulterers—or even like this tax collector. I fast twice a week and give a tenth of all I get.' But the tax collector stood at a distance. He would not even look up to Heaven, but beat his breast and said, 'God have mercy on me, a sinner.' "I tell you that this man, rather than the other, went home justified before God. For all those who exalt themselves will be humbled, and those who humble themselves will be exalted." (Luke 18:9–14 NIV)

After reading through this parable, I am made aware by the power of the Holy Spirit of the importance of humility in our hearts. Our love for God is increased when we are aware of our own need for God's forgiveness. This awareness, combined with humility, compels us to humbly ask God for his mercy. This is a profound principle that our Savior teaches us in this parable. We as people are all in need of God's mercy; we cannot grade ourselves worthy to God solely because of our works.

A high-minded attitude puts us in jeopardy of being blinded by pride and feeling we no longer need his mercy. This prideful attitude in our hearts is a destroyer of humility. The Lord taught us that the tax collector went home justified by God because he humbled himself. He showed humility before God in his heart. The pharisee was the opposite; he lacked humility and boasted of his own works to God.

This parable teaches us about God's perfect justice and our own need for his mercy. His glory and work come before us and our works. This is a hopeful teaching for me while here in prison. I am humbled by my circumstance and have nothing to boast about. The paradox is an eye-opener and a beginning for wisdom—even sinful mistakes in our lives can be a catalyst to turn away the selfish pride that once blinded us. In the gospel of the Holy Bible, the works of Jesus Christ are being proclaimed. He saved us by his own blood; what could be more humbling than to accept him and to share in his sufferings?

Surely, even those who are in good circumstances are still in need of God's mercy. Humility is a place in our hearts from which we can approach God and receive his Son. We are prepared in humility to be taught by Jesus Christ all the word of our Lord. Somehow we are brought to the awareness that everything is prepared for us by God. With these principles in our minds, there is no place for pride to take root.

"He is before all things, and in Him all things hold together" (Colossians 1:17 NIV).

This scripture reveals something very hard to receive: without God's work being done first, there is no one able to fully repent. God the Father reconciled all things to himself in the sacrifice and the resurrection of Jesus Christ, his only begotten Son. He did this so the wrath of perfect judgment we would have been required to endure was completed by his grace.

> For God was pleased to have all His full-
> ness dwell in Him, and through Him to rec-
> oncile to Himself all things, whether things
> on earth or things in heaven, by making
> peace through His blood, shed on the cross.
> (Colossians 1:19, 20 NIV)

God made peace with us through the blood of his Son, his only perfect Son. This is God's grace given to the believer. This very same grace is why the tax collector in the parable went home justified by God.

Jesus told us the parable of the tax collector's prayer as an example of a repentant heart. The tax collector's repentance was not that of works or actions but rather it was exemplified by his prayer, "Lord have mercy on me." His repentance was in his heart. His humility was in his acknowledgment of God's sovereign power. The tax collector did not aggrandize or admire himself in any way. The pharisee, on the other hand, was an example of an unrepentant man. In his pride, he did many good works. The Lord did not count any of his works, he could not be justified by his own works. Very simply, the pharisee did not focus on God's work. His prayer was focused on his own works, efforts, and exertions in comparison to other people. He was not directed in humility toward God and his perfect power.

By telling us this parable, Jesus teaches us the quality of humility so that we may know the nature of repentance. Repentance is not an obstacle course we must run through suc-cessfully—an obstacle course where we may become distracted by how well we perform compared to other competitors, an obstacle course in which we begin to become proud of our own performance and begin to believe our own work is what repen-tance is. In its essence, repentance is turning to God's mighty power to save us. It was God's most masterful work that reconciled us to him, not our work that reconciled him to us.

> Once you were alienated from God and were enemies in your minds because of your evil behavior. But now He has reconciled you by Christ's physical body through death to present you holy in His sight, without blemish and free from accusation. (Colossians 1:21, 22 NIV)

If we fall into the trap of defining repentance as a collection of our own works compared to others, we become just like the pharisee. In this sense of our own pride, we cannot be justified by God. When Christ tells us the parable, the tax collector begs for God's mercy in faith. God's perfect Son counts the tax collector's faith as *righteousness*.

Jesus knew that he was on earth to fulfill the whole law of God. He would even fulfill it unto death on the cross so that all who believe in him might be saved. By the grace of our perfect God, I understand that all that needs to be done first in order to repent is to accept and believe in God's perfect work through his Son, Jesus Christ. This parable is to teach us that a repentant heart has faith in God's work for us and in God's perfect faithfulness to us.

When we receive a testimony of Christ, we have repented. And now, God's work "in us" becomes righteous through our faith in Christ. Just like the tax collector, we are justified by God, and we live in his grace and mercy.

> "Come," He said. Then Peter got down out of the boat, walked on the water and came toward Jesus. But when he saw the wind, he

was afraid and, beginning to sink, cried out, "Lord save me." Immediately Jesus reached out His hand and caught him." "You of little faith," He said, "Why did you doubt?" (Matthew 14:29–31 NIV)

We receive from the Lord the mercy and faith that we ask for immediately! In conclusion, the Lord's perfect faithfulness to us and our reception of it is repentance. Strive as we may to do good works; when we focus on anything other than our Savior, we begin to sink as Peter did on the water. The parable of the tax collector and the pharisee praying at the synagogue and the story of Peter walking on the water are very different. Both stories are profound depictions of the essence of repentance. They describe two very different men in two completely different ways, looking to the Lord to be saved.

The pharisee was unfortunate in his pride; he divided his faith between Christ and his own works. He was not saved by God. When Peter allowed the storm to divide his faith in Christ, he began to sink into the water. Just as the lowly tax collector who God saved because he asked for mercy, Jesus also reached out to Peter and lifted him. Peter and the tax collector—both imperfect sinners, both obviously not focused on their own actions, abilities, or works—were saved! God's perfect faithfulness to them was given because they both looked to him to be saved. In this, we learn the amazingly simple truth, God's own power to save is repentance for those who reach out in humility to his Son, Jesus Christ.

This means the righteous works we do are done through Christ's power. Just as Peter did not walk on the water by his own power or his works but walked by Christ's power, we also can walk by faith. We can be counted righteous by God's work and faith working within us. In this faith, we know our God and live in the love of his spirit as truly repentant souls. The fear of God is now replaced with love. Any doubt we may have because of what we may have done or even our current sins and issues are not a hindrance to God's perfect grace.

> This is how love is made complete among us so that we will have confidence on the day of judgment; In this world we are like Jesus. There is no fear in love. But perfect love drives out fear, because fear has to do with punishment. The one who fears is not made perfect in love. (1 John 4:17, 18 NIV)

CHAPTER 5

Testify of Christ

The most important influence in the life of a born-again Christian is the Savior Jesus Christ. With Jesus Christ in our minds, the glory of God is his. He will enliven and invigorate our minds to testify of him with our mouths. When the Holy Bible has been examined in a vigorous study by the believer, it is powerful to destroy harmful illusions. Many of the snares of sinful delusion and illusions of all kinds once prevailed in our lives. The lies and schemes of the devil and his followers are what the gospel equips us to prevail against. This is the spiritual war against all evil; we are now those who fight the good fight.

In our lives as Christians, the devil seeks to steal away the blessings and gifts that God provides to us. He does this with lies, schemes, ideas, and information in opposition to the Word of God. It is a war that we are asked to fight, not a physical war but one that is of a spiritual nature. The information that is from the world is in many cases an attack against God's Word, especially when it opposes God's will and repudiates the truth of Jesus Christ's resurrection.

When the Holy Spirit of God is present in the life of the believer, the wisdom of this corrupted world is an offense to the indwelling spirit. The cynical wisdom of modern hysteria and pomp becomes obvious as being of little or no value except for evil. Our heart, spirit, and mind cannot make progress in the spirit of God if it is fed with worldly information. Worldly wisdom and the hype of modern ideas and factoids are not the good work of God. The scriptures are the manna from heaven, and so much of this world's information is the manna that will spoil and rot. Both the desire for the Word of God and the power that comes through Jesus Christ are bestowed upon us because of his faithfulness to us. His faithfulness to us is displayed in the gospel of the Holy Bible.

All of this world's ideas, information, and wisdom are far from God's supernatural strength and power. We are God's children, and we do not progress by his guidance unless we both seek and obey his Word. We must remember it is all God's work from the foundation of Jesus Christ's sacrifice and all he will build up from there. Jesus Christ becomes our guiding light. He equips us with all of his most valuable tools to enable us to overcome any evil in our way.

The vital power contained within every word of our Savior's mouth blesses all who place faith in him. In this, his spirit of truth and power, there is safety and rest for us. The knowledge of our salvation is now a testimony in the darkest places; our testimony is a light source to those still enslaved by evil in this lost world. We are the light in the darkness for all who need the saving grace of Jesus Christ to give them hope. Our faithful testimony can bring life to a suffering soul in spiritual darkness. The testimony we carry is one of the most powerful tools we have as disciples of Jesus Christ.

It is the testimony of Jesus Christ upon our mouths that brings the Holy Spirit in all of God's power to change the hearts of the unsaved. In the power of the Holy Spirit, we can be the bravest souls winning glory for the almighty God of salvation. What an amazing gift we have! We are those who share the supernatural love of God. As a man in prison who knows very well the pain I felt before being saved, I can rejoice in the opportunity to share what I have been given. With the joy that comes from service to God, there is no despair. Worship and service, when coupled with study and prayer, bring a depth of well-being to my heart. These basic principles are invaluable treasures that we can share with everyone who is drawn by God to hear the message of Jesus Christ.

In the effort to be prepared to share the gospel through studying, the spirit of God gives us the power we need for our minds and spirits to be attentive to his will. There are many miracles still yet to be done, and our Savior holds all of them in his hands. We can take hold of him by faith, and he can give us the wings of an eagle to fly through any spiritual storm. With his spirit, the shape of our lives miraculously changes. Where once there was a desolation, now we can see the green pastures of bounty and abundance. Hopeless thoughts no longer prevail in our minds; every dark, dead idea is supernaturally transformed into life. Our hearts are no longer defeated, nor can they be.

There is no defeat that can destroy you with the Holy Spirit to strengthen your resolve to stay in the faith of Jesus Christ. The battles and struggles are now the mountains soon to be removed by faith. We as new children of God in his faith have been given the assurance of the most infinite and awe-inspiring blessing to reign with him in glory, to know him in every way. He is the creator of all things; with him, all things are possible.

To the weak and broken, the words of our Savior are not only the inspiration but have the literal power to heal us. I pray for all who read this book that the Savior be alive to them as he is to me. The story of who Jesus Christ is, is no longer just words written on a page, but they are brought to life through the Holy Spirit and carried by people from all walks of life, from diverse nations and languages by the power of God's spirit to the entire world. When we speak to bless and heal this world and the people in it, he is always with us. His spirit within us beckons us to share joyfully the gifts we have received.

Believers are hope-filled people who share hope with everyone. When the dreadful day of fear is upon us, we rejoice in faith, knowing God's spirit goes before us to prepare the way. The grace of our King is enduring and everlasting. He will send his holy angels to help fight against the evils of this world. We have provision beyond anything this world can provide. God's hand is upon all that we do in Jesus's name.

Freedom is in the arms of our Savior Jesus Christ. The chains of fear are broken. I write these things for the power of our Savior to be made known to people who feel unworthy of his love.

The past sinful events of our lives are forgotten and remembered by God no longer. This principle of God's truth is a barrier against backsliding. We press forward, and no evil can destroy the new heart God has restored. Demons and devils tremble at his name! All of Satan's most desperate attempts to erode our joy are easily burned away by God's holy fires. His holiness and faithfulness to us is a purifying fire that no evil can withstand. Grace is God's perfected love for us in Christ. We no longer have any debt that hasn't already been paid by the blood of the perfect lamb!

Even as our hearts and minds are being changed, God's spirit within us heals all the wounds of the human soul. We have been bound up with him, raised from death to life with him, sealed to him, and justified because of him. Our lives are his, our bodies are his, and his spirit is forever present. When the world of evil surrounds us, we celebrate to show the glory of God to those who are lost. Raise our voices to the King of Heaven, and proclaim his holy name. Share our love with all we can as Jesus gave freely of himself to us; we also share freely of ourselves.

The hearts of all of God's children are joined together with him, united by the Holy Spirit, to bring light into the darkness. With our arms wide open and our minds renewed, we become the salt that saves. We can stress the value of his faith within us. By the words of his gospel, we can assure others of eternal life to all who are fallen into a depth of sin and despair. Every single soul is of the utmost importance, and all can be made useful to God through faith in Jesus Christ. The gospel principles can bring purpose and hope to people who truly are the downtrodden and redeem them who are victims of sin and who are overwhelmed with guilt.

> But when the kindness and love of God
> our Savior appeared, He saved us, not because
> of righteous things we had done, but because
> of His mercy. He saved us by the washing of
> rebirth and renewal by the Holy Spirit, whom
> He poured out on us generously through
> Jesus Christ our Savior. (Titus 3:4–6 NIV)

This miracle of God's grace is for everyone to hear! It is an inspiration for prayers in the power of the Holy Spirit to declare victory over all Satan's efforts to destroy. We do this in obedience to Jesus Christ who asks us to pray for our enemies. His love for those who are dead in their sins is alive in the heart of the man transformed in faith.

When all else is lost and there seems to be no rest in the life we live, grace from the King pours out upon the soul that thirsts for Christ to speak to him. His life force is the substance that holds all of creation together, with him, through the fierce torrent of hatred, malice, greed, and evil judgment. This power is both for us and for the blessing of our enemies. The most awful of this world's evils are not the invincible walls we are confined behind. Jesus Christ was the victory over all Satan's schemes intended to destroy us.

> Having canceled the charge of our legal indebtedness, which stood against us and condemned us; He has taken it away, nailing it to the cross. And having disarmed the powers and authorities, He made a public spectacle of them, triumphing over them by the cross. (Colossians 2:14, 15 NIV)

In this world where there is so much to discourage a person and so many obstructions to progress, the failures of our lives push up into our hearts to destroy hope. The value of faith in Jesus Christ is unequaled. The logic of the world would try to exert itself to add confusion in an effort to deteriorate the merit of his perfect power. He laid down his life intentionally by surrendering to the cross. He was raised to life again, and he walked once again with those who had known him. That is how he disarmed all of this world's authority. Death and even hell itself could not contain him. When his faith within us is active, the spirit of God is also within us to work in all of the worlds around us for the same purpose and disarm all the authorities of darkness and any power that fights against Christ. His victory is complete, and it is the ageless and ever-present power of life itself.

"See to it that no one takes you captive through hollow and deceptive philosophy, which depends on human tradition and the elemental spiritual forces of this world rather than on Christ" (Colossians 2:8 NIV).

When we are made aware that Jesus Christ is the head of every power and authority, the testimony is alive in us to experience his peace. The horrors that would otherwise disarm us begin to have no effect. The worldly dread is no longer a forceful attack to bring us into fear of anything. Nothing can bring any fear to Christ. He is the head of all who abide in him. It is a walk by faith not by what we see.

In the vision of our physical eyes are all the worldly visible things; this is a way for the devil to gain so many strongholds. It is our God, Christ, the spirit of God who sees and knows all the invisible things. His force is prevailing always in the heavenly realm in every way and for his father's purpose. The blinding effect of spiritual evils is completely disarmed by him continually. The truth of his might in our father's power is only contested by things of this physical world. In the spirit, there is no power that can contest his sovereign power. There is no other power in all creation that rivals his. He has the supremacy in all things.

"And He is the head of the body, the church; He is the beginning, the firstborn from among the dead, so that in everything He might have the supremacy" (Colossians 1:18 NIV).

CHAPTER 6

A Leap of Faith

With the trials of our lives upon us, we are asked by our God to follow him through his Son. The spirit of the Lord is our teacher as we take our journey by faith. We cannot be the one who is fearful and shrinks away from the unknown future God has prepared for us. Faith is active as a living tool within us when we follow God with our hearts. This fellowship with the Savior is what has taken my own worldly ideas out of the way. His power to lead us into the unknown is what a walk by faith is. With Jesus Christ the king of heaven and earth, there is absolutely nothing in the way.

His spirit goes before us in power to open brand-new doorways into new horizons. He prepares revelation for us in *his keys* of wisdom to walk in faith, perceiving spiritual realities. Discernment brought to life in his spirit. The real miracles of Jesus Christ are being done inside of the man who walks by faith, making his power active for God to use. He speaks the words of truth within us, quickening us to leave *our own purposes* behind and to be swallowed up in his purpose for us. We are enabled, empowered, and given purpose to do amazing things in his hands.

Supernatural power proceeds us, and with God's unrivaled power within us, even the demons tremble. There is no longer any pathway into the darkness that he does not go before us to shed his light upon. His power is in force; life is the substance of his work. We walk in the footsteps of the King; no worldly authority or organization can thwart him. With such an awesome faith, the power he holds is a light even within us, and our hearts are full. The illicit troubles we *perceive* in the spiritual attacks against us, as well as in the physical world, are incapable of changing God's purpose and direction for us. The storm of evils has no power to change the outcome of battles in our future. They have already been won by Jesus Christ.

Keep in mind, in Jesus's very own life, he proved by word and action that there was no enemy capable of destroying him. He still lives, not only within us but also in all his creation. If his power is for us, then our destination is with him. He is the literal way to heaven. His life is eternal life; we are his friends, and we are the sons and daughters of God. What evil worldly limitations can ever be placed upon us? What evil worldly limitations could ever be forced upon him? He did no evil, so what can ever get in the way of his plan for us?

With the faithful Son of God to go out before us and to provide for us, the walk of faith becomes an abundant life. We can speak of things that cannot be seen and have confidence in God to bring them to pass. The world that we are in is in the hands of God. He reigns in perfect glory from heaven above. Even the earth trembles and is in motion by his power. Faith is truly his, and we are gifted by him to have it. Jesus Christ is our servant when necessary and our good shepherd, who is perfect before God. He gave his life to God to gain our victory from death and hell. The chains in our life are easily broken when we agree with God that his Son already set us free.

> Jesus replied, "Very truly I tell you, everyone who sins is a slave to sin. Now a slave has no permanent place in the family, but a son belongs to it forever. So if the Son sets you free you will be free indeed." (John 8:34–36 NIV)

We can confidently follow the Lord through all battlefields—fires of doubt, storms of evil—without the stain of fear in our hearts. His own spirit will know how to prevail for us. The power of his light within us forces out the shadows of fear and doubt; no confusion will be left. In whatever we endure or whatever comes against us, his spirit is victorious over all things. The prisons of the world have been torn away by him. We cannot be again enslaved by God's enemies or ever be destroyed. Where he was the victorious one, we are his victory.

He paid every price, every spiritual debt to purchase us back with his own blood. We hold in us his power to be healed and his power to save by the perfect name written upon our hearts. God looks down on us and sees us as the perfect righteousness of his own Son. Our lives are transformed from the inside out, and the world around us conforms to his will. His power to change all these world's obstacles into blessings is manifested as we follow him. His message through us shed abroad through the Spirit is the supernatural work of God for all creation to hear. There will be no obstacle to prevent his work in you from being done for the blessings of all people to hear of God's promise for those who believe.

He protects those who proclaim the salvation of the people through Jesus Christ's sacrifice. We are justified to proclaim that all who believe are seen by God as justified in the resurrection of God's Son. There is no other purpose among men than to proclaim the work of redemption through Christ. It is God's immortal will that the message of Christ be our most prized possession. The beauty of his loving embrace is spoken to all who are yet to know him. His spirit is a fire to invigorate the minds and heal the souls of every human being who receives him into their hearts. What more noble a purpose in all this world than to testify of Christ's power to save a person from sin and evil and Satan himself? To save people from their depraved minds, broken spirits, and the living hell they are in without Christ. The power of his spirit pierces into the heart of those who are cold and dead. To those whose lives of painful suffering while blinded by Satan feel that they are already dead.

This is what God's work is to save us and to bring God's life to the spiritually dead—people who are dead inside and feel like walking and talking zombies in a world with no peace and only pain. The Spirit carries us forward and puts the testimony of Christ into our mouths to save those who are spiritually dead, not just lost but dead! The life of Christ is the healer within us that gives us life. The birth of his spirit to the dead brings them into his life. All joy and love—every good thing comes from him. This is the essence of our Savior to those who walk by faith.

His truth blazing like fire within us through his spirit casts out evil spirits, and we begin to tear down the strongholds of Satan by the power of his Word. This is what the walk of the faithful disciples of Jesus Christ is, bringing the testimony of his Word to everyone who will hear it. This is what abundant life is in the hearts of all who are saved.

How abundant is the substance of peace to people who have never known God's peace or any peace for that matter? He gives peace to people who feel only pain in their hearts and minds. That is the abundant life of peace now from within. In the walk of faith, we go along with the Savior to bring life, freedom, and hope to the devil's slaves. We go forward with his keys to unlock every person that is a slave to sin by faithfully sharing the gift we have been given.

His gift of perfect freedom and love is more powerful and of greater value than anything else on earth. Redemption is now ours to share; we are the people who are saved from our own slavery of sin and shame. Our own degraded lives of sorrow and regret were taken away from us by Jesus Christ. He has replaced what he took from us with uplifting grace and filled us with peace and happiness. We now make the Savior's power known to all who will hear his message! His faithfulness to us is perfect; we do not need to fear our own weakness. The stone we once would have held to throw at whoever had offended us has been taken; our hands are clean as we bring blessings and love to them. The damaged heart that once shared grief and pain and brought with it more suffering to the world around us is now healed.

His grace is more than enough to prepare and sustain us to go forward in peace. Abundant life begins in the wealth of God's spirit within us and brightens the once negative attitude that was a force of destruction. Abundant life *in him* is the awareness of the mercy of our God alive within us, which sets us free from the jaded, cynical, narrow-minded, critical, and blinded opinions and judgments that destroy happiness.

In the walk by faith, we can become people who are cleansed by him to understand what perfect liberty is. He is the liberator of us all to deliver us from Satan's power, to defile us. The brightness of his perfect love drives out the devil and breaks his power that brought fear into our hearts. Our lives are now in *his life*, and the devourer who would destroy or bring us the fear of death has already been beaten by our Savior Jesus Christ. Christ was raised from the dead to prove that death had no power over him and also to show the faithful it has no power over them.

> Since the children have flesh and blood, He too shared in their humanity so that by His death He might break the power of him who holds the power of death—that is, the devil—and free those who all their lives were held in slavery by their fear of death. For surely it is not angels he helps, but Abraham's descendants. For this reason He had to be made like them, fully human in every way, in order that He might become a merciful and faithful high priest in service to God, and that He might make atonement for the sins of the people. Because He Himself suffered when He was tempted, He is able to help those who are being tempted. (Hebrews 2:14–18 NIV)

Without the living word of Jesus Christ to embolden our hearts, we are left vulnerable to our sinful desires. What the conqueror Jesus Christ has done for us is a sustaining bridge to carry us over the chasm of death that we could never cross without him. Worldly fears of poverty, oppression, and the despair that is the result of hate, anger, turmoil over earthly substance, war, government corruption, ethnic burden, historical evils, and all things that bring about the anguish of our souls in Christ—these things are the defeated works of Satan in the world. In the life of our Savior Jesus Christ who shares no part of the darkness whatsoever, we too are the light that cannot be defeated by the power or authority of his fallen world.

"The Lord will rescue me from every evil attack and will bring me safely to His heavenly kingdom. To Him be glory forever and ever, Amen" (2 Timothy 4:18 NIV).

In our own mortal fears about our bodies, finances, security, the condition of our communities, and national standings, all the anxious forebodings of mortality, through the power of his faith within us, we are now dead to all of these worldly travails. When the inner man is reborn by his spirit, he is buried and becomes dead to worldliness. We are lifted into his abundance. We testify to all creation of his eternal life and the fires of his Holy Spirit alight upon the darkness of this fallen world. His mighty power is the guiding glory of our own testimony.

His power to save is what is ultimately important, and our walk by faith is the invisible bridge over the chasm of death and hell that we choose to walk over! We are now inspired and given power to push forward with courage as we preach in unchartered territory. We become aware that all we endure—whatever we may suffer—and all that we do is for the glory of God. Personal vain ambition, prideful notions, and the hardship of confused hesitation fall away in the walk by faith. The hysteria of this world's confusion and doubt peels away by God's only begotten Son as we follow him.

We would have once been like Peter, distracted by the storm; we are transformed by him in the walk by faith to be solely focused upon our Savior. He lives his life with us, and the evils of this world surround us with no power to corrupt us. The firm indestructible foundation of Jesus Christ will never crumble or fail us. Our physical lives are made joyful through all hardship because the indestructible God of all creation made us his vessels. This is the abundance of God's love within us—a solution more absolute than any human effort could ever provide. What personal ambitious work could I possibly do that leads to perfect peace? The pathway to perfect peace is Christ the King. His ambition is to do the work of God.

When the wisdom of our Savior is present in our minds and with his love, the deafening sound of all of Satan's kingdom is blocked out. What would have had the power to stop us is now being moved out of the way by God. Negative emotions and vain plans that would have crippled us are made into clear pathways as the spirit of God cuts a road through our own personal jungle of disillusionment, disappointments, setbacks, and struggles. They do not stifle us any longer! We take faith in the unknown plan of God's efforts in our lives and take joy in the journey.

> Remember those earlier days after you had received the light, when you endured in a great conflict full of suffering. Sometimes you were publicly exposed to insult and persecution; at other times you stood side by side with those who were so treated. You suffered along with those in prison and joyfully accepted the confiscation of your property, because you knew that you yourselves had better and lasting possessions. So do not throw away your confidence; it will be richly rewarded. You need to persevere so that when you have done the will of God, you will receive what He has promised. For, "In just a little while, He who is coming will come and will not delay." And, "but my righteous One will live by faith. And I take no pleasure in the one who shrinks back." But we do not belong to those who shrink back and are destroyed, but to those who have faith and are saved. (Hebrews 10:32–39 NIV)

So with the words spoken to us of those who have gone before us, we find confidence in the walk by faith. Taking our offenses out of the way is what God has done for us. We can go forward with a clear conscience. The past is no longer an enemy *within us* to take us into Satan's captivity. With faith in Christ, we are free to enjoy life without the onslaught of regrets, shame, and negativity taking away from us the joy of today. We are being made rich by God, our inner person being prospered beyond comparison.

Contentment is no longer a distant goal to struggle for. Abundant satisfaction and peace of mind are what Jesus Christ can give us, no matter what the situation. His prosperity is ours to be held in our minds, hearts, and souls. His abundant life to us heals the afflicted soul we once suffered.

What we once had, what we want, where we will be, what we missed, what we never had, when we were hurt, who was wrong and who was right, what we failed to do better, who failed us, who did we fail—why this, why that? These are all worldly sorrows that lead to death. Like a pig back to the sty or a dog back to its vomit, Satan attempts to turn our attention to these things so we will begin to wallow in them. The spirit of God beckons us from the inside to flee these things. With the spirit of God to testify to us that we are those who have been given eternal life, we see an awesome gift that is distinctively the very essence of the cup that runs over and the epitome of the quality of abundant life.

When *his life* is the focal point of our heart and soul and we give our bodies to him for his purpose, all that we have been given is his as well. Today, as well as every day, is a day of renewal and rebirth. A Sabbath day of rest and freedom in the truth of God's grace is exactly what the new covenant affords us—every day! We have been blessed to have his grace all the time, not only on the Sabbath day! If the scriptures have become the *living word* within you, you have been quickened by the spirit of God; and your journey is now being built upon the sure foundation of Jesus Christ. He is literally the Word of God alive within us.

"In the beginning was the Word, and the Word was with God, and the Word was God" (John 1:1 NIV).

As the Word of God, Jesus Christ begins to reinvent and restore our minds, hearts, and souls; and we become more like him. This is why we are called new creations; we are born in the Holy Spirit to be remade in every needful way. Have you ever heard any scripture from the Bible about God or Jesus ever having any kind of discussion complaining about how much either one of them did wrong, forgot to do, or planned to do but just did not see it happen? I can promise you that regret over what they could not accomplish is not a part of scripture.

Our human condition is one of frailty, weakness, unmet expectations, broken dreams, and broken families. I can assure you the dreams and visions God has for you—in his family—cannot be the failed plans and lives we *feel* we have been experiencing, simply because it is not God's nature. Perfect God, perfect plans, perfect results. Without exception! The hopeful person who places faith in Christ will gain life. When we give up *our lives* for his sake, we find our lives; when we choose to keep our lives for our own sake, we lose them.

This selfishness and pride are the reason for so much of the sorrow in our hearts over all the frustrated efforts and plans we have not accomplished. In pride, our lives are truly already lost. The surrounding circumstances of the world, no matter how good or bad the events may be, are made joyful when we accept God has prepared them. If we are prideful in our own efforts to work hard and selfishly gain momentum, we then find ourselves hungry even though we expect to find satisfaction. In a sense, we turn from God's grace; and the selfish vain life we create is a heavy burden.

I don't know what you have done or what you have been through in your life, but the Lord does know. He knows your heart's desires, deepest pains, fears—everything. When we give our lives to him, he saves us from the inside out and in every way. When we try to save ourselves, we destroy our lives from the outside in because we can only give ourselves the excess from our own human baggage, along with the excess human baggage from the world around us. Success, money, status, and all else can never really accomplish what God can do inside of our hearts, minds, and souls. The walk with the Savior is fulfilling long before any of the accomplishments develop. That is why it is a celebration of simply knowing our Savior.

When you are already full of happiness and feel good despite any adversity because of his love, you can only be blessed from that point forward. If you make outstanding progress and succeed greatly, then you are blessed by it. If you make no great advancement and have additional hardship and struggle, you are already joyful throughout because the Lord gives you his grace through it all. Jesus Christ is the sure foundation for a happy, strong, courageous person to build upon. From there, God does the building, and what he builds will always stand. This is the promise of God to all who are drawn by the Father's spirit to receive his Son into their hearts.

A transformed life begins on the inside and reflects outward. All the while, the real power of God is manifested all around us. A sure foundation is a primary need for the miracle to happen. This truth is the primary purpose of the gospel of Jesus Christ to the world.

CHAPTER 7

A New Perfect Purpose

"But if we walk in the light, as He is in the light, we have fellowship with one another, and the blood of Jesus, His Son, purifies us from all sin" (1 John 1:7, 8 NIV).

We make a choice after receiving the Savior to continue to be with him in the very same light. This is the purposeful pathway that powerfully redefines the attitude of our hearts. Bitterness toward others and grudges that would otherwise inevitably lead to isolation, even depression, are covered over by the faith in Jesus Christ's sacrifice. This brings us back into joyful fellowship with others. Friendships can grow closer in God's light than ever before. When the regret and sorrow that would evolve in our friendships because of sins are covered over with faith in Christ and God's love, we begin to forgive and understand people in a brand-new way.

This opens doors for us in our lives. We have intimate relationships that are healthy because of Christ. In the light of our Savior, the natural tendency to judge harshly is tempered with mercy. With the knowledge of our own sins before the Lord and humble confession, our character changes from natural action to spirit-filled resolve. The betrayals against us are now new opportunities to forgive and love as our Savior has proven his love for us, even to lay down his own life for us. When we are convicted of our own sins and the Spirit awakens our minds, the gospel of salvation softens our hearts. We know God's mercy, and we feel his love for us. This compels our new life in Christ to be a vibrant, meaningful, and hopeful life. His compassion for us inspires compassion for others. Faithful principles take root in us, and virtues begin to grow.

Freedom from anger is the gift God gives us when we live with forgiveness in our hearts. Angry, critical, shallow attitudes full of indifference, and pride destroy friendships while patience and mercy develop friendships. The source of all good things, Jesus Christ, is the perfect example that prepares us to be those who share in his righteousness. The Savior is our peace; when *his* peace is sown into our hearts and minds, we begin to make peace with others. The perfecting power of God's spirit within us promotes personal and relational well-being. We receive goodness from God, and what we give out is an outpouring of the wealth God has given to us.

As the pathways of our thoughts and actions are made straight, a new *well-being* that is from God develops strength where there was once a weakness. While we begin to reap the benefits of what his spirit instills within us, that very same light precedes us and is reflected back at us. We learn to trust in him more and more as his blessing is realized in our lives. The hopeful prayer of faith in things yet unseen becomes the reality of blessings we have now been given. And the truth of Jesus Christ's promises to us is made real in our lives.

"Until now you have not asked for anything in my name. Ask and you will receive, and your joy will be complete" (John 16:24 NIV).

What a *miracle* it is for me to be in prison amid such evil and sorrows and yet to be one who has a joy that is complete in Christ. The inner man that I am, to my utmost heart and soul, is being provided for in every way by the Savior. My circumstances, however hard they may be, are now joyful. Transformed by the hand of God, my wounds are now healed. I testify that all believers can receive the very same healing in their lives. It is love from God that infuses itself inside me; this grace carries me, and it is this perfect love that will sustain every faithful heart drawn to Jesus Christ.

The ideas in our minds because of sin and our natural human nature, which once stood against us and brought us into conflict with ourselves and others, are removed by God because of what Christ did for us. We are no longer removed from God's wealth of peace, virtue, and well-being.

> Once you were alienated from God and were enemies in your minds because of your evil behavior. But now, He has reconciled you by Christ's physical body through death to present you holy in His sight, without blemish and free from accusation. (Colossians 121, 22 NIV)

The inner turmoil of the heart and mind—the destructive force that causes despondency in our souls, making us hostile to others because of opinions or combative in our attitudes, even against ourselves—has now been cured by faith in Jesus Christ. This promise of the gospel is transcendent; it supersedes our own sins because the removal of our offenses was done for us by God. We are now those who have been given his favor, and we have a clean slate in his eyes. Knowing this and keeping our hope in God brings the love of *his* healing power to others as we share the testimony we have received.

This testimony is the light in the darkness to those who are lost. Human wisdom, human works, human philosophies, human kindness, or even human love are not capable of restoring a person to God—simply because all of our efforts are imperfect, which means no matter how much better we do in our actions, we are helpless to stand in God's favor without Christ. The accolades of accomplishment and the acceptance gained by climbing the ladder among our peers cannot clear the slate between us and God.

The inclusion within our communities and any blessings gained are made into fulfilling, satisfying, and uplifting experiences because of Jesus Christ's life within us. Our new hearts are made whole by him, and the mind of the faithful disciple is free to enjoy life without the inner turmoil and conflict constantly interfering with contentment. This is the evidence to us and others that glorifies our Savior. When our ambition is to bring him glory, the transcendence of his spirit carries with it the virtues he exemplified in his life. The power of God's work being superior to any of our own establishes humility.

Where egotistical ideas once turned our efforts into vain ambition, the spirit of God now keeps us humbled. We don't act in our pride, so we are protected from the pain and confusion we once felt when our pride was wounded. All of these blessings in our hearts, minds, and souls stem from the gospel of Jesus Christ. The person reconciled to God through Jesus Christ is now able to be spirit-filled and fully prepared by God for good works.

There may still be many struggles and all sorts of adversity, hardships, and trials. This world is packed full of them, but with the gospel of truth as our guide, we can endure and be hopeful and full of joy in every situation.

> I know what it is to be in need, and I
> know what it is to have plenty. I have learned
> the secret of being content in any and

every situation, whether well fed or hungry,
whether living in plenty or in want. I can do
all this through Him who gives me strength.
(Philippians 4:12, 13 NIV)

This is an outstanding source of comfort. God's powerful Word within us is infinite even though we are only people; the infinite God is within us. We grow up in his infinite, powerful, and awesome spirit. With such an abundance of good tools and directions, the man who is born-again has at his disposal resources more reliable than any worldly knowledge could ever provide. God's provision is what the disciple is promised. God's provision is beyond the secular professions and divisions of this world. The blessings and provisions of our God are infinite resources able to restore broken lives, save communities, and even heal nations.

All the nations of the earth are blessed through Abraham's seed. Our faith in Christ is a restoring power to all of the earth. Now that is an extremely unrestrained provision given to the born-again Christian who chooses to share the gospel of salvation with everyone who will hear it. His spirit is with us as we sow the seed of his Word into the people of this world. He promised us that if we stay in his presence, all things can be overcome. His Word will always carry with it the provision of the infinite almighty God.

"But you will receive power when the Holy Spirit comes on you; and you will be my witnesses in Jerusalem, and in all Judea and Samaria, and to the ends of the Earth" (Acts 1:8 NIV).

CHAPTER 8

Powerful Provider

We are provided for in every way the power of God before us, within us, and behind us. This faith in God's provision is capable of indestructible transformations in us and the world around us. His provision for his purposes was to bring freedom to the weary people held in slavery to tyranny and break chains of poverty throughout the world. The living God of our testimony bears witness to the truth of freedom in Christ, giving us the power to proclaim our transition from slavery and death into the richness of God's life. The Holy Spirit makes provision for the seed of salvation to be planted in people's hearts. The smile on the face of just one new believer, someone who now has hope that they have never known, is more rewarding than all the paychecks in the world. Our own lives begin to shine in his glory as we continue to know him in a more intimate way. In the word that was spoken through Christ for all who have been called, there is refuge supplied and fortified with every good thing for every good purpose.

"But seek first His kingdom and His righteousness, and all these things will be given to you as well" (Matthew 6:33 NIV).

In every word of our Lord, there is wisdom and direction to amply provide for us. We can have confidence in the Mighty

One and his Son, Jesus Christ, to be victorious in this world and every evil in it. With that as the foundation we build upon, we too overcome, and we begin to prevail instead of fail. When we prevail over this world and its evils, the lost and hopeless are invigorated and inspired. One believer shares with the next what has been freely given, and God continues to pour out more and more provision upon those who serve him. He is always with us, and he knows the struggles we face; and his hand upon us in life is for the purpose of his will to be done.

We know our purpose in life as we continue to follow him. He gives us the provision to be outstanding in the gifts, talents, and special skills needed to accomplish his purpose. These talents and special skills shine bright in his glory as we are built strong both individually and collectively. Always remain faithful to him to accomplish his purpose with the strength he gives us to press forward even when there are obstacles, resistance, and great adversity acting in opposition against our Savior's message of salvation.

"Now Lord, consider their threats and enable your servants to speak your word with great boldness" (Acts 4:29 NIV).

The encouragement contained in the scriptures for us to be made bold by faith is provision for the weary soul. When the born-again Christian is constantly eating the manna that came from heaven, the Word of God, the Savior's uplifting provision, carries us when we would otherwise fall. At the very same time, the Holy Spirit touches the lives of those around us to lift them with the very same provision when otherwise they might fall.

"You are the salt of the earth. But if the salt loses its saltiness, how can it be made salty again? It is no longer good for anything, except to be thrown out and trampled underfoot" (Matthew 5:13 NIV).

We are the salt that saves because our Savior is the Word of God; his words are kept, and we speak them into the world. With his words, the power of faith is within us.

"The Spirit gives life; the flesh counts for nothing. The words I have spoken to you—they are full of the Spirit and life" (John 6:63 NIV).

We are persecuted but not destroyed. We rejoice in the afflictions we endure, knowing we have the promise of a much greater reward in heaven. So while we follow our Savior, we pray for our enemies. We pick them up even as God has lifted us. This is God's awesome provision given through the Word to the lost. Not only are we boldly inspired to share the testimony of Christ, but we are also given the power to overcome. The sins of our former lives—the sins that had blinded us and knocked us down—are no longer the destroyers they once were in our lives. This is the verifiable truth spoken by God's spirit directly to us from within when the chains of sin are broken in our lives. When we speak the Savior's words of freedom and truth, the Holy Spirit carries the message of God's victory within us to those who are still suffering from sin.

This is the very real, tangible manifestation of our Savior's power in a world in so much darkness. This is how a born-again Christian shines bright and becomes the lamp put up on a stand to light up the whole house.

"Neither do people light up a lamp and put it under a bowl. Instead they put it on its stand, and it gives light to everyone in the house" (Matthew 5:15 NIV).

All the inspired good deeds we can do are done for the purpose of glorifying our God. His light shines through us as we proclaim his Word. God's awesome infinite provision is given for the blessing of all heaven and earth through his faithful ones. Who is a good Christian? The one who is faithful to overcome. But who can overcome sins in their life? The person who is born again in Christ, who—because of his faith through us—knows God's provision is salvation, redemption, and justification. We continually learn he is able to help us overcome them. He has provided for us.

"For everyone born of God overcomes the world. This is the victory that has overcome the world, even our faith. Who is it that overcomes the world? Only the one that believes that Jesus is the Son of God" (1 John 5:4, 5 NIV).

We have both the blessings, anointing, and promise of God to be those who are gifted to overcome all destructive forces and sin with the provision of our Savior Jesus Christ. As the life we live is made a victory through Christ, we become more than conquerors. His faithfulness to us is perfect and cannot be compromised by any evil at all. He won the victory over sin, and we are given victory when he lives within us. By his spirit and his Word, we are made clean.

In this walk of faith, a man like me—a prisoner, a sinner—begins to have the most important and profound epiphany: I am really no longer myself! What a beautiful conundrum, I am no longer angry, anxious, critical, confused, depressed, lonely, hopeless, and full of fear! I lost myself to the Lord, to the Word of God in the scriptures, to prayer, to worship, and to love! Should I be mad that all of the characteristics that once made me *me* are now mostly gone? The *me* foundation could never have brought his faith to life or righteousness in me! My own transformation is shocking to everything I once thought was *real!*

There is such an awe-inspiring transformative power in the Holy Bible. His faith coming to life within me through the scriptures has done something for me more effectively than anything in this world ever has! The Word has absolutely changed me, and my outlook is absolutely different because I have been changed! My emotional scars, depression, and anxious yearnings are gone because my heart has changed!

The anxious yearnings I had for people to do or to be something for me have been changed into a heart full of the Savior's love to give freely. The soul that once went from confusion to hostility to mystery and illusion is now changed into a confident temperament, full of well-being, and free from mystery and illusion. The truth of the gospel—all God's faithful Word, being heard and made alive inside of me—has made me into a brand-new person!

"Therefore if anyone is in Christ, the new creation has come: the old is gone, the new is here" (2 Corinthians 5:17 NIV)!

The tedious and seemingly impossible task of identifying all of my problems—then trying somehow to solve the immensity of complex issues, trying to free myself from the tangled web of anguish built over my lifetime—has all been done in a rather short time, all in a very peculiar way, simply by reading the Bible and putting the words of it into practice. The ineffective absurdity of all my past efforts to change my life without being born again are now revealed to be the illogical and unreasonable vain efforts done in my weak human strength! Only by the blessing of God's spirit—his gift to us, directing us by the scriptures—do we have any capacity to understand the Word of God for his useful purpose in us.

"The person without the Spirit does not accept the things that come from the Spirit of God, but considers them foolishness, and cannot understand them because they are discerned only through the Spirit" (1 Corinthians 2:14 NIV).

The word of our Savior is the life-bringing power to bring redemption to all who will hear. We are so very blessed to be in his grace! Inside of us—through the Word, God's purpose, Jesus Christ—lives to continue to fulfill God's plan, save people from horror filled lives, free them from a defiled and awful existence, and bring us joy and hope. The promises of our Savior to the world are God's most important purposes within us. So we are transformed by God in order to be prepared to carry his light to all that he is preparing to receive his salvation!

"But thanks be to God, who always leads us as captives in Christ's triumphal procession and uses us to spread the aroma of the knowledge of Him everywhere" (2 Corinthians 2:14 NIV).

This is the exact purpose of the work God is doing with supernatural provision throughout the world. It is the primary reason that I have been transformed by him and given discernment in the writing of this book. His faithful testimony to this world, in power, is always the catalyst for change. As a man who is a prisoner, completely without the outside world's approval, I am saved to do his work. This means the transition from uselessness into meaningful and unrivaled purpose for God to make provision and to justify.

In the worst moments of my born-again Christian life, confessing my sins, I am no longer a man dead in those sins. Instead, I am a man who is alive in Christ to share his message. From a foundation as perfect as the gospel of truth, the life I live as a prisoner—even for my violent crime—is no longer a life in vain. In Christ, I can no longer be a person who dwindles away in hopelessness to a dark and bitter end. The gospel is before me to bring light into the darkness of any path that lies ahead.

So very powerful is the Lord in all of his might, we too are made powerful with him. What terrain could possibly be too treacherous for God to traverse? In this encouraging faith, the mountains are moved for *his* sake. Many, many people are affected by the faithful testimony of someone who has placed all their trust in Jesus Christ. As we are compelled by him in our lives, the miracles of *his life* within those who are around us is done by the Holy Spirit's supernatural power.

"For we are to God the pleasing aroma of Christ among those who are being saved and those who are perishing. To the one we are an aroma that brings death; to the other, an aroma that brings life" (2 Corinthians 2:15, 16 NIV).

The Word of God will deliver those who the Father prepares to hear it from the awfulness of life in vain. To those who accept Christ, the gospel becomes a brand-new life of promise and abundant hope. To those who are too proud or too full of human wisdom to receive the redemption God provided through Christ, our testimony represents death to the perishing. There are those who will perish and will be left to dwindle in darkness and die in vain. My life in Christ is not one of shackles and chains even while incarcerated. The Lord provides me liberty and freedom. It is the everlasting, eternal freedom, and it has been given to me right here in Arizona State Prison Complex Yuma, Cibola Unit!

"Now the Lord is the Spirit, and where the Spirit of the Lord is, there is freedom" (2 Corinthians 3:17 NIV).

The spirit of freedom is a supernatural tool in our lives to help set free the hearts of those who are enslaved by any evil, whether it is their own sin or the evils in the world surrounding them. The message of our Lord Jesus Christ, in the Holy Spirit's power, is the ultimate force of God to set people free. When a new believer is set free from the chains upon his heart—mind and soul by the Word of God—his promise of freedom to him is the new salt they begin to share with those around them. Christ has the power to save all of God's creation, only those who refuse his life-saving sacrificial love will be lost.

CHAPTER 9

A Pathway of Prayer

In our new life—Jesus Christ within us—our desire for prayer is more profoundly compelling and more consistent. As a born-again Christian is a new person, with a new heart, the Spirit begins to pray with us according to God's Word. Prayer is now open in a new way to those who have been made to understand they are the temple of God. Inwardly, God's ever-present eyes are upon us, within us and our minds, hearts, and souls. We are in powerful communion with Jesus Christ. We are his; the pathway of prayer is now open to us to know heavenly virtue. We are made able to constantly pray with the Spirit for renewed hearts, either with our mouths or inwardly.

This is of the utmost importance here in this world, where evil is in constant attack against our Savior; and we, too, are targeted by the devil continually. In the gospel of Jesus Christ, his undeniable life and resurrection, he proved absolute power to bring all of Satan's attacks to an end. He did this in the spirit of God by prayer and with the words of his mouth. He is the only begotten Son of the indomitable God of all power—as Immanuel, the fullness of the Father became flesh. His Word dispelled the attacks of Satan succinctly and with no exception.

In the pathway of our prayer with Jesus Christ, inwardly praying with him, we are those who are constantly defended by his Word against all of Satan's efforts to destroy. The devil had no power to destroy our Savior, and he has no power to destroy the prayerful saint who is spirit-filled in full communion with the Lord. There is absolutely no contest of wills between the enemy and Jesus Christ who has won the victory over Satan. In the knowledge we have through the Holy Spirit because of the Savior, discernment is real. We are not empowered by an intangible idea of hope that is only on some distant horizon. We are filled by his Holy Spirit. It is with us right now and forever!

We are made able to stay on a pathway of prayerful communication with God and constantly be fed by his Word. This prayerful pathway in his spirit will bring peace to us and others as we go through the spiritual storm. In the power of God's spirit, Jesus Christ is the eagle that fought its way from every enemy, sin, temptation, demon, and evil storm. He did this flawlessly and was raised from death to perfect victory! This was done to bring the knowledge of God's victory to us so that in Christ, he could also bring us through the very same storm.

In our hearts, his pathway of power is firmly planted; and in the pathway of prayerful communion with him, our minds are minds that can be directed to fend off the enemy. There is no other way through the storm of evil that our world is so entangled in spiritual evils, physical depravity, immorality, pestilence, illusion, despair, and misery after misery. This storm of evils can easily ensnare and potentially destroy the new born-again Christian who neglects prayer. The seed of God's Word can be stolen away if the newborn believer does not remain prayerful. We must be compelled by the Holy Spirit to remain in the pathway of prayer and always remember that the cares of this world are the spiritual storm that surrounds us all.

Suddenly a furious storm came upon the lake, so that the waves swept over the boat. But Jesus was sleeping. The disciples went and woke Him, saying, "Lord, save us! We're going to drown!" He replied, "You of little faith, why are you so afraid?" Then He got up and rebuked the winds and the waves, and it was completely calm. The men were amazed and asked, "What kind of man is this? Even the winds and the waves obey Him!" (Matthew 8:24–27 NIV)

What are we in the storms of this life if we forget to stay in the pathway of prayer faithfully knowing Jesus Christ can calm every storm? We are those caught in the middle of the storm who will drown. He is powerful to do *within us*, the very same thing he did in *the physical way* on the lake with his disciples. He can make the storms that are so very prevalent in our lives be rebuked by his command. His life and Word within us, as we are sealed to him by the Holy Spirit through God's promise, has made the pathway of prayer powerful to rebuke the storms we are bound to go through.

The pathway of constant inward prayer, relying upon his Word, immerses us through the Holy Spirit with the faith that was made perfect. Although our own minds and hearts are fallible, his faith within us is perfect to calm every storm. This means that through prayerful searching of the scriptures, the inward prayers of our hearts are now his words. He can prove to us the very same thing he proved to his disciples on the lake. He rebuked the storm that brought them to fear. This is what our Savior is able to do for any of us. With his immutable prayer of faith within us and with his Word to prevail against the storm, there can now be a place that is completely calm.

That place is God's rest—his perfect peace—which has made its home to reside within us. The Lord is the peace and the rest for our minds, bodies, and souls. There is no anxiety, restless energy, confusion, trepidation, worry, depravity of the soul, or any disturbance that could ever shake the Savior. Jesus Christ, through the pathway of prayer, is the provider of God's perfect peace to us.

> Listen then to what the parable of the sower means: when anyone hears the message of the kingdom and does not understand it, the evil one comes and snatches away what was sown in their heart. This is the seed sown along the path. The seed falling on rocky ground refers to someone who hears the word and at once receives it with joy. But since they have no roots, they last only a short time. When trouble or persecution comes because of the Word, they quickly fall away. (Matthew 13:18–21 NIV)

When Christ spoke these words to his very own disciples there, it was of profound importance to them. There is a divine purpose in every word that Jesus Christ ever spoke. As a new person who was born again because of his Word, I can attest to the value of knowing every one of them. The prayer in the heart of the believer—with Christ's word filling our minds and the Holy Spirit to testify with us—is the prevailing force that assures us we remain in Christ. This prevents the seed from being snatched away or falling away because of persecution. Jesus Christ and the Holy Spirit who teaches us will make us able to know all that is necessary for a freedom that is beyond anything this world could ever begin to provide. God provides an inward solace and peaceful refuge so perfect that it can only be described as immaculate.

The Savior Jesus Christ himself is the immaculate conception of God's spirit brought into the world, the living breathing Son of God. Weight the new birth of the Savior's faith within me, I know very well that the parable of the sower was intended for me and all other new believers of her to take heed. The darkness in this world—spiritual evil and tyrannical power—is so very prominent in all that surrounds us. Anyone who has ever begun a new walk in Christ goes through them. Troubles and all sorts of persecutions will be part of the testimony built within us through Jesus Christ. Whatever trouble is brought against us by the enemy of God, the deceiver and destroyer of our minds, hearts, and souls comes upon us like an awful storm.

Jesus Christ will rebuke the storm, and there will be a complete calm when we choose a pathway of prayer, using his sacrifice and his Word as a helmet in our salvation being secure. The assurance of salvation by the blood of Jesus Christ is imperative for the new believer to remain and continue in the faith.

"But the seed falling on good soil refers to someone who hears the word and understands it. This is the one who produces a crop, yielding a hundred, sixty or thirty times what was sown" (Matthew 13:23 NIV).

We are brought from death into life with our Savior Jesus Christ to be those who will produce a crop of lost people being saved. We are coworkers in the field with Christ. We are alive in his Holy Spirit to bring our testimony of God's work of salvation into this world.

The test of our faith by the enemy of God—the persecutions, etc.—is Satan's effort to prevent us from faithfully producing a crop of new believers alongside the Lord. Satan knows we can never do as the Savior asks of us if he can stop us from sharing our testimony of Christ.

"Through Jesus, therefore, let us continually offer to God a sacrifice of praise—the fruit of lips that openly confess His name" (Hebrews 13:15 NIV).

The gospel is built solely upon one sure foundation—his own sacrifice for us—to be bought by his blood, to be redeemed, and to be justified. God's grace provides faith to believe that salvation came through Jesus Christ's sacrifice. This is the sure foundation that must be testified of as we share the gospel. We know and bear witness that salvation is secure because of what the Savior experienced in going to the cross.

This assurance of salvation is the *helmet of salvation* the apostle Paul spoke of in Ephesians chapter six. He knew all too well what the storm of this world was and still is because he had been prepared in Christ to endure it. This is what the great apostle Paul described for us to know the cause we have been chosen for as believers in Jesus Christ.

> Finally, be strong in the Lord and in His mighty power. Put on the full armor of God, so that you can take your stand against the devil's schemes. For our struggle is not against flesh and blood, but against the rulers, against the authorities, against the powers of this dark world and against the spiritual forces of evil in the heavenly realms. Therefore put on the full armor of God, so that when the day of evil comes you may be able to stand your ground, and after you have done everything, to stand. Stand firm then with the belt of truth buckled around your waist, with the breastplate of righteousness in place, and with your feet fitted with the readiness that comes from the gospel of peace. In

addition to all this, take up the shield of faith,
with which you can extinguish all the flam-
ing arrows of the evil one. Take the helmet of
salvation and the sword of the spirit, which is
the word of God. (Ephesians 6:10, 17 NIV)

This passage is a very elaborate way to draw a person's attention to Jesus Christ, to bring about sincere trust in God. The apostle Paul wrote this to encourage you, who received Christ, to love the Lord and trust him with all of your mind, body, soul, heart, and strength. It is not really a symbol of the soldier for his outerwear, it is a way of highlighting the importance of honoring the Lord with your whole person. This is for anyone who has been born again by the Spirit and by water. We are the children of a mighty God who asks us to give him our trust entirely.

The pathway of prayer in Christ between us and God is the very essence of putting on the whole armor of God. We, as his faithful people, dedicate all we have to him. Every implement belongs to Jesus Christ. He is every piece of the armor. He is the faithfulness of God Almighty to us. He is the righteous one of Israel. He is God's perfect truth. He is God's perfectly obedient begotten Son. He is the Son of God and a peaceful teacher that remained silent while scourged. He surrendered perfectly to God in death to assure salvation was won for us. He is the man the Holy Spirit descended upon as a dove. He is the living Word of God!

And you also were included in Christ
when you heard the message of truth, the
gospel of your Salvation. When you believed,
you were marked in Him with a seal, the
promised Holy Spirit, who is a deposit guar-

anteeing our inheritance until the redemption of those who are God's possession—to
the praise of His glory. (Ephesians 1:13, 14
NIV)

We are all included in Christ when we believe in his message. The Holy Spirit of promise is a deposit that guarantees the
inheritance of eternal life with God. Our prayer lives are now in
the eternal life of Jesus Christ within us through the promise of
God. We are the inheritance in the hand of the mighty God of
all creation. Paul's description is implying the inner spirit of the
man quickened by the principles of the Holy Spirit brought to
life as we follow the pathway of prayer, applying all of them as
we walk with the full armor of our Savior Jesus Christ. There is
ample provision, endless inspiration, and constant communication from Jesus Christ to his faithful believers.

We gain unparalleled protective armor when we simply
focus our prayer lives, thoughts, and ambitions *on him*—the
Word of God. Jesus Christ, our own and only almighty King, is
the power by which all creation was formed. In this glory, our
new prayerful hearts are sealed to him by the Holy Spirit. This
is the purpose of Paul's very distinctive elaboration of the armor.
It is so profound and yet so simple, we pray in the power of our
God. His glory upon us and his Holy Spirit within us is that
armor of every kind.

As a born-again who knows the power of prayer in Christ,
I testify as Paul once did of our almighty God's power. We are
able to be grateful in all things because God's blessing is for
us. We are to give thanks to him constantly in prayer. We can
know the person who our Savior Jesus Christ is personally. The
principles of his faith are written upon our hearts because of his
work done to us. We can learn to use the pathway of prayer for

the sole purpose of being in remembrance of him and united in principle and purpose.

He is perfect righteousness, so in our inward prayer, we thank him for his life and for renewing and transforming our hearts and minds. This will bring the faithful, useful purposes of God's righteousness into our lives. With love shed from our hearts, he is our breastplate of righteousness because righteousness comes from faith in him.

"So also Abraham 'believed God, and it was credited to him as righteousness'" (Galatians 3:6 NIV).

If our hearts are his and we are faithful in our belief in his Word, the breastplate of his righteousness will guard our hearts and prevent us from being deceived by fear or doubt. The breastplate of his righteousness protects our hearts as we push through the evil in this world. In order to give us fortitude and persevering power through the most deplorable and heart-wrenching experiences, this uplifting strength brought to us through the Holy Spirit within us is the principle upon which our personal refuge is built—a personal refuge that protects us going through the potentially evil and character-defaming world. It guards our character and gives us joy through what otherwise might lead to the shriveling of our hearts' capacity to grow in the love of our Lord Jesus Christ.

"So those who rely on faith are blessed along with Abraham, the man of faith" (Galatians 2:9 NIV).

We can now understand faith with the heartfelt sincerity of Jesus Christ. He was the perfect faithfulness of our God. God's own faithfulness and love are expressed to the whole world in the life, sacrifice, and resurrection of Jesus Christ, our Savior.

"But God demonstrates His own love for us in this: while we were still sinners, Christ died for us" (Romans 5:8 NIV).

With the pathway of prayer *in him*, the Holy Spirit inspires us to faithful remembrance of his Word. Our prayers in his

Word bring his purposes to light, and the grace of God is a perfect armor for our hearts. So in the testimony of faith, I am guarded against the heartfelt despair that comes from tragic loss. My heart is protected from the hateful schemes and ambitions of this world. The devil is condemned, and he has been conquered by the Savior on the cross of Calvary. Our prayerful hearts made whole by him are now led by the Holy Spirit to be filled with enduring love.

Forgiveness becomes easy to do. Resentments begin to fall behind us, and we are full of good thoughts. With our hearts renewed, we are emotionally prepared to testify boldly of Christ's saving power. Our hearts begin to burn with a hopeful desire to share his message. We are full of desire to share the joy that we feel! True happiness, evident to all, resounds within the chambers of our hearts with an outpouring of love to share with others. Paul's purpose in the elaborate description of the armor directs our prayers to Christ to focus our purpose upon him and his truth. The truth was the very first part of the armor mentioned—the belt of truth. In truth, we can be courageous to speak of Christ without hesitation. We are proclaiming the name of Jesus Christ in the power of his Holy Spirit!

What an amazing gift to both us and anyone who hears his truth! We no longer have to be confused! We never have to be timid in sharing his message of God's truth. It is being done in his supernatural power through the outpouring of the Holy Spirit. We can be given many gifts and talents through the Lord. His Father is the God that provides abundantly in every way. With the living truth of Jesus Christ inside us, we are prepared to share it with everyone!

The cup of his loving kindness runs over. The Savior is the epitome of perfect peace. The storm on the lake that brought fear to his disciples did not even wake him up!

His word within us is forgiving and full of merciful love. Salvation is God's to give, and we share in it through Jesus Christ. This changes the nature of our hearts to reflect his peace outwardly. With our prayers focused on him—who he is, filled with the principles of his faith—we stand in the presence of God. This increases the peaceable fruit of patience, and in peaceful waves, we are uplifted to praise him with our voices. Remember to keep in mind that he is the God that lifted us. When we remain in faithful prayer and trust in the Lord for peace, we are made to know real peace—made and remade! We are transformed by the renewal of our minds! This peace we are *made* to experience transcends the trivial aggravations and fruitless strife that come at us in full force from a world full of proud arrogance. The Spirit's fruit of peace dispels the hostilities and puts an end to the inner turmoil that is projected at us from all of the miseries in the world—whatever they may be, no matter how insignificant the issues or how important the problem is. That peaceable fruit is developed through yielding our prayers to the Holy Spirit and following the admonitions of the gospel.

In the wisdom of the Holy Spirit, the apostle Paul draws our full attention to Jesus Christ as a prayer incentive. Think of it as a prayer meditation. For instance, we are given Jesus Christ's faith when we believe in him because of the change in our hearts. His faith is *born* in us! Jesus Christ is the exactness of what Paul envisioned as the shield of faith. His own blood is the shield that protects us from all the enemies of God. There is absolutely no enemy that has the power to destroy the heart of our Savior. He is able to defend us against every offense that would otherwise discourage a man from walking in the Holy Spirit. This is an offering of the Savior to us. His blessings are upon us; they precede us into any firestorm.

Then Paul inspires the Ephesians to consider the promise of God—the assurance of the salvation that was secured for them and us by the blood of the Lamb. The perfect Lamb of God—he is the salvation upon our head. There is no deceiver that can ever erase what was done on the cross for all who are drawn to the faith. The faithfulness of Jesus Christ is available to all who are drawn to him by the Father's spirit. The Savior is our perfect, indestructible helmet. The salvation of our King is the free gift of God. No other price ever needs to be paid to ransom us from sin, anyone reborn in the Holy Spirit of God.

There does not need to be any doubt of his power or his purpose—he is the Redeemer. We remain prayerful to know we are completely saved from any evil. Hell cannot prevail against Jesus Christ the King. With a heart made alive in him, knowing we are in the Holy Spirit of our God, the sword of perfect truth goes before us to cut away any of the devil's efforts to destroy. Jesus is the Lord who goes before us into heaven itself. His victory is what we also enjoy in this life. In every situation with thanksgiving. Jesus Christ, the perfect Word of God, is the sword to destroy the storm of illusions, deception, lies, deceit, and treachery of the devil. His victory is *complete*!

> Do not let your hearts be troubled. You believe in God; believe also in Me. My Father's house has many rooms; if that were not so, would I have told you that I'm going there to prepare a place for you? And if I go and prepare a place for you, I will come back and take you to be with Me so that you also may be where I am. You know the way to the place where I am going. (John 14:1–4 NIV)

CHAPTER 10

The Whole Measure

Personal opinion or understanding does not affect the truth. For instance, if all I have personal knowledge of is a three-inch miniature ear of corn, that does not make it a large ear. It remains a three-inch miniature ear of corn although it may be the largest ear of corn I have ever seen. Truth is king and prevails over perspective. For example, to an ant, a three-inch miniature ear of corn would be many times larger than its own one-quarter-inch body. The perspective of the ant does not have any power to redefine the three-inch miniature ear of corn into a thirty-inch ear of corn. The three-inch ear of corn remains unaltered whether it is seen in my hand through my eyes or as a giant seen through the eyes of the ant.

In the righteousness of God, there is only *truth*. Truth is not a diplomatic presentation to appease the ear of the listener. Truth is absolute unbiased knowledge or fact regarding a place, event, or thing. In truth, there is no exception. In truth, individual perception does not alter it as fact. In other words, the three-inch miniature ear of corn remains a three-inch ear of corn although it may appear to be large in comparison to a one-inch ear of corn. Truth is perfect, and opposition to it is futile. A variable of perfect truth does not exist. The one-inch ear of corn is not altered in size by opinion, neither does a different increment of measure change its one-inch size. Sixteen-sixteenths of an inch is still one inch. Although the change in the incremental measure does have the power to alter perception, it does not change the length. The exactness of the truth, although changed numerically by the increment of measure, remains the exact same length.

For a Christian, salvation is a perfect eternal truth—the Word of God—to those who hear and receive him. Our own faith in his Word could be likened to any of the variables based on each individual's measure of faith and maturity. Personal opinion, experience, perspective, and bias are all active forces in us as human beings. We, as individuals, may have a wide range of information that may be in opposition. In other words, my own perspective on salvation defines what it means to me. Inevitably, the same applies to all believers. For example, I have knowledge and testimony that incorporates opinion, perspective, experience, and bias. It is fair to say that all believers have a testimony containing these human character traits as well.

The truth of God's Word and the promise of salvation to us as believers is perfect. His truth cannot be altered by our opinion. The opposition created between one believer and another when the measure I have been given appears to be different from what my brother in Christ has been given. The truth of salvation through God's promise remains the same.

For example, when I measure salvation by the one-inch measure of faith and works as opposed to my brother's sixteen-sixteenths of an inch measure decided by their faith, works, tradition, and ordinances, the truth of God's salvation remains the same. Salvation is not redefined by us at all; we, on the other hand, are being redefined by salvation.

Our opposition to one another between believers is futile. The illusion created by differing opinions, experiences, perspectives, and biases does not change the nature or measure of salvation. In other words, each believer has been given a measure of faith and righteousness. One believer, as an ant to a three-inch ear of corn, perceives salvation as enormous in size; and another believer, as a mature adult to a three-inch ear of corn, perceives salvation as a small matter. Salvation from one perspective to the next is different in its appearance because the measure of one believer to another is different. Righteousness is from God. The truth of Christ as a sacrifice demands that salvation remain the same. Salvation remains the same regardless of what measure we, as believers, are given.

When I measure salvation at one inch and you measure salvation at sixteen-sixteenths of an inch, we are redefined by righteousness in the Holy Spirit of God to know that salvation remains the same perfect truth. Our tools of estimation and our own faith in God have the measure of righteousness God has given to us individually. The perfect unchangeable truth of God and the fullness of God's righteousness are complete in Christ Jesus. The promise of salvation is through him, and the measure we are given is from him. And the opposition we once perceived is swallowed up in him. By the Holy Spirit, we, of different measures, are brought together as many pieces of the whole—the body of Christ. One salvation, one God, one family. The sons and daughters of God have been given the name of his Son, Jesus Christ, upon us. This is the whole measure of truth and righteousness.

CHAPTER 11

Blessings through Trials

In our Christ-centered lives, the power of God's Word is the key to our faith. As his disciples, we are profoundly changed by the Holy Spirit. The testimony of Christ, now alive within us by the power of the Holy Spirit, beckons and compels us to walk in his will. The power of God to speak to us through the written and spoken word becomes understandable. The purposes and directions of God, as Christ and his disciples spoke them, are now discerned by the Holy Spirit within us. We are blessed to be the people that are in Christ as he remains in us. We are always invigorated by him to persevere through any trial we face!

It becomes a joy to do all that he has asked of us and continues to ask of us. His life is essentially being formed with us with the power of God. All that once seemed impossible to persevere and overcome becomes possible.

"I can do all this through Him who gives me strength" (Philippians 4:13 NIV).

I would like to make the truth of this scripture speak to us with power. What is the nature of our God if it is not the very nature of Christ himself? As he is formed within me and you, our minds, hearts, spirits, and bodies become more like him.

The transformation is real! When once in our lives we became overwhelmed by problems that came against us, now the joy of Christ is with us.

We now share in his victorious life. God's wisdom is within us to help us examine and overcome adversity. We reach into the scripture and write it upon our hearts, and the Holy Spirit quickens our thoughts and fills us with immeasurable grace— grace to love even through the most difficult times in our lives, to forgive even the worst offenses, to change hearts around us, and to preserve us in the trials we endure. This is the nature of Christ who lives within us, becoming our *new nature*.

Amazing gifts are in our thoughts, and the character of our spirits is made alive in Christ. We can bring to God the brokenness in our lives. Our sinful thoughts, actions, wrong deeds, and persecutions we may endure—all can be brought to the Lord for his mercy and comfort to renew us. We can have the perfect presence and power of God's own Son, made by our High Priest to offer us perfect consolation in his redemption and his sacrifice for all these things. We can be in his rest, all this from within us as we draw strength in the Holy Spirit.

"But He became a priest with an oath when God said to Him: 'The Lord has sworn and will not change His mind, "You are a priest forever"'" (Hebrews 7:21 NIV).

So as Christ's disciples, the promise to us is a complete perfect sacrifice for all sins. He is alive even through us to intercede on our behalf. This brings contentment to the believer who is alive in our Savior. He can meet our innermost yearnings and restore our emotions, as well as make us upright in our spirits when we begin to lean or even fall.

"Therefore, He is able to completely save those who come to God through Him, because He always lives to intercede for them. He lives forever to intercede with God on our behalf" (Hebrews 7:25 NIV).

This is a profound and amazing truth of what our God has done for those of us who are blessed to be in his Son—the perfect power of God, even to take upon himself our sins, in his Son Jesus Christ. The struggle we once had to make peace with all of the pain caused by our sins has all been wiped away by the new life of Christ within us. This brings an indescribable peace without boundaries, giving me a transcendence from the small-minded travail and grief by filling me with hope. In the presence of our Savior, the joy is complete and sublime. All we need to do is ask, believe to receive, and live to achieve.

"Until now you have not asked for anything in My name. Ask and you will receive and your joy will be complete" (John 16:24 NIV).

The resounding power that comes with the new covenant to us is the continual renewal of our hearts, minds, and spirits as we are constantly having all of our needs met by Jesus Christ.

"Such a high priest truly meets our need—One who is holy, blameless, pure, set apart from sinners, exalted above the heavens" (Hebrews 7:26 NIV).

With our Messiah to make all this possible for us even from within us, we know how to be joyful and content. When we are persecuted and scorned by people in awful ways, we are not compelled to be angry, mean, or judgmental. Instead, the grace of our merciful God is already awakened inside us to give us loving kindness toward our enemies and to those who still wish to do evil to us. This is the Holy Spirit making us into the image of God's own Son. We literally become the lights in this world.

"And we all, who with unveiled faces contemplate the Lord's glory, are being transformed into His image with ever increasing glory, which comes from the Lord, who is the Spirit" (2 Corinthians 3:18 NIV).

In a personal study and prayerful pondering while studying God's Word, the Holy Spirit speaks in living volumes. A literal amplification of the Holy Spirit's living testimony and truth comes in wave upon wave of thundering understanding being brought by God's Word to my soul. This awakening is liberating and dispels many false judgments and alleviates assumptions brought about by my ignorance. The awareness of God's Word is the resounding assurance of the whole symphony of life that completely dissolved the dead illusions in my mind and my heart. The Holy Spirit testifies to me his power to unite us in the body of Christ.

The Holy Spirit transcends the boundaries of socioeconomic class distinctions and the border of ethnic, national, historical tradition, and aesthetic convention to bring about a family united in love.

The body of Christ is colored by differences in language, tradition, and worship practices as diversified as only a god-sized body could be. The Holy Spirit speaks to all of us, forming a common bond through our belief in Jesus Christ, our Savior.

The gift of God is the treasure of heaven to open the eyes of the blind.

LOOKING GLASS

As I read about You, In your everlasting glory,
The angels rest in silence near my side
Oh, Holy Lord
My song is given to You,
With a heart that is down and lowly
I hear the promise of Your Son
As He calls out to me
With loving words adoring
And promises me the blessings.
Of an everlasting life!
Oh, my Lord, I adore You,
And I give everything for You,
But all I have left to give,
Are these lonely dreams and ashes?
And the dust left on the glasses.
So, I hit my knees,
And I pray tonight.
Oh Lord please take my life.
Take me away, oh take me now to that land of milk and honey.
To that stream of living water
That can't be bought with money.
And open up my eyes.
Open my eyes with the light.
Of Your infinite glory

Let Your Spirit go before me.
As I walk in the newness of this life!
With a brand new heart
And a brand new start
With the angels by my side!
Let me look upon You in the looking glass.
With Your mirrored image placed before me
And I gaze into the fires of your eyes.
And let Your Spirit rest upon me.
With an open face beholding
Even as I am changed into the very same image.
From glory to glory
Even as by the Spirit of our God

Erin Daniel Bryant